In Case of Emergency, Break Glass

In Case of Emergency, Break Glass

Pearls of wisdom to bring you back to yourself

Bryce Kennedy

2020

Cover Art by Roxy Faridany

ISBN: 9798559632162

Independently published

To Bridget, may we always find the northern lights together.

Table of Contents

III. YOUR TRUTH   106

IV. YOUR FREEDOM — 148

Introduction

"*Life should not be a journey to the grave with the intention of arriving safely in a pretty and well preserved body, but rather to skid in broadside in a cloud of smoke, thoroughly used up, totally worn out, and loudly proclaiming 'Wow! What a Ride!'*"

Hunter S. Thompson

In the early spring of 2014, I had an emergency. As it so happened, this burnt-out, stressed-out, overeating, drinking attorney had several bleeding stomach ulcers. It became painfully obvious when my stool was jet black and I had barely the strength to get out of bed. Who would have guessed?! My lifestyle seemed like such a picture of health: 80-hour work weeks followed by long nights at the bar.

Once I got the diagnosis, I sat on the edge of the bed and stared out the window of my 396-square-foot studio apartment and knew this couldn't last. This wasn't the life I wanted. Living to work. Numbing out. There had to be more. Somewhere inside me, I knew something had to change, rapidly. That's when I decided to "break glass."

In Case of Emergency, Break Glass is a book to help you overcome difficult situations in your life. To go beyond the limitations of those situations. It is to help you re-discover the part of yourself that can overcome any adversity. The part of you that is the tool, the cure, the answer to any and all problems. Just like one of those ubiquitous In Case of Emergency red boxes we see in buildings that can aid us when we are in trouble. Inside it, an axe, fire extinguisher, first-aid kit, hose, or, for very serious emergencies...a bottle of whiskey. All we have to do is break the glass and use it.

Once I broke the glass, life changed very rapidly. I embarked on a period of self-exploration. Questioning everything. Reading everything. I ultimately left the practice of law and devoted my life to personal transformation. There was so much I didn't know. Spirituality, belief systems, samskaras, breathing, meditation, and more. I wanted to know Truth. What was influencing my behavior and thoughts. I wanted to see why I was so affected by other people's reactions. Why I spiraled in high pressure situations. Why I was so sensitive. Why I wasn't owning my bigness. Why?!

I needed an outlet to share all of the information I was discovering, so I began writing a blog called Bryce's Grand Experiment. You see, Bryce's Grand Experiment was not prosaic legal dictum, it was about something deeper. It was about the major transformation, awakening, and upheaval going on in my life. To write that was absolutely terrifying. But I wanted to share with people the realizations I was having so they could expedite the end to their suffering. Avoid the mistakes I made. I wanted them to find happiness. Love. Fulfillment.

Soon, the blog grew and I was writing every day. And as it grew, people started asking for help. It started off with a few consultations but eventually became my full-time job. Since then, I have launched my consulting company and I have been fortunate enough to work with people from all over the world and from all different walks of life. I then branched out to corporate coaching, primarily because of Boston Consulting Group. They hired me on a whim, which led me to become the in-house coach to hundreds of their consultants. It opened the doors for me to work with many new companies I previously wouldn't have had access to. By breaking the glass, I completely transformed my life.

However, it was always a goal to speak with more people and share on a broader scale. Which leads us to *In Case of Emergency, Break Glass*. This is a compilation of everything I have learned while helping people get unstuck, find themselves, and be bigger. The book is six years' worth of my writings detailing my adventures in transformation, beautiful client stories, spiritual and mindfulness theories, impactful quotes, and a little bit of magic.

This book is a bit different. It is meant to be read as you see fit. It does not need to be linear. I structured it so it could be flipped open to any page and read with no other context

needed. It is loosely divided into four parts. Your Power.
Your Choice. Your Truth. Your Freedom. These are the core
themes of this book. And under each part, there is a pearl of
wisdom. 77 in total. These pearls are meant to be tools in the
box. The ones you retrieve when the glass has been broken.

It is my sincerest hope this will help you when you need it
most and that you always remember…

In Case of Emergency, Break Glass.

Love,
Bryce

I. Your Power

#1 Fuck The Rules

"I am free, no matter what rules surround me.
If I find them tolerable, I tolerate them; if I find them too
obnoxious, I break them. I am free because I know that I
alone am morally responsible for everything I do."

Robert A. Heinlein

There was my client, standing under the archway of the 2,035-year-old Temple of Dendur in the Metropolitan Museum of Art, staring at me. I was about 100 feet away staring back at her.

We could not break eye contact for ten minutes. I was timing it.

There were hundreds of people trying to take a picture of the archway with the temple behind it. And smack dab in the middle was my client blocking the most prized photo opportunity in the entire museum.

The rules were simple: No looking away. No apologizing to anyone. No uncomfortable laughs. No fidgeting. Just uninterrupted eye contact.

See, my client was the type of person who was a major success at work but, in her personal life, it was a different story. She didn't like to take up space. She didn't like to make people feel uncomfortable. She didn't like to feel vulnerable. She didn't like to be seen.

She didn't like where her life was headed.

But my client was an incredibly special person. She had an amazing heart. Beautiful power. Deep care. She just forgot that these qualities still existed in her. It made sense. People had hurt those parts. They had taken advantage of them. It was easier to hide.

So, we didn't hide. We put her front and center. She was going to own the temple like the goddess she was even if it killed her.

Prior to this, we had been working together for weeks. Slowly and delicately allowing the hidden parts to be seen. Allowing them to have space to breathe. Allowing an opening to the vulnerability and pain. Allowing them to be heard. They began as a whisper but grew to a roar.

And she was ready to embody her power.

As she walked up to the archway, winding through the crowds, she began sweating. She tried to negotiate a shorter time. What if people got mad? What if she got kicked out? What if?!

There were enough "what ifs" in her life.

There were enough unspoken rules she had to live by that she never chose.

We began.

1 minute: Fear. Terror. Legs buckling. The holy shit moment.

3 minutes: Wanting to apologize. To look away. To run out of there! All of her programming was coming back. Don't be big! Don't take up space! DON'T!

5 minutes: The world cracked. It was all silenced. A surrender. A shift. A calm taking over. A density.

7 minutes: She was unmovable. She was a pillar. She was open.

10 minutes: She was total.

When I waved to her that we were done, she didn't move for a few seconds. She had become one with the temple. She owned it. It was her space.

It was the last step in rediscovering who she truly was.

She came over to me smiling. She was different. She was radiant and confident. It took guts to piss off hundreds of people, but she did it.

She was able to break through all the mental chains and shackles that were imposed on her throughout her life. She broke the layers of fear and judgment. She broke through the falsity.

Essentially, she broke the rules that imprisoned her.

We all have these rules. Rules that keep us small. Afraid. Hidden. But once we make the choice to shift and move through them...we start to live. We are free. We are big.

After it was all over and we were walking out of the Met, I asked her what it was like to stand in an area where she shouldn't have been standing, blocking all of those people, taking up that much space, breaking the rules unapologetically.

She laughed, looked at me with a fierce fire in her eyes, and said,

"Bryce, fuck the rules."

#2 Life Begins When Identity Ends

"It's the basic condition of life to be required to violate our own identity."

Philip K. Dick

As the fates would have it, in a brilliant and humbling cosmic joke, we humans, the top of the food chain, share 60% of our genetic makeup with a banana.

21% Welsh, 19% Irish, 60% Banana.

It's true. Now, let it sink in. Because this can either be extremely liberating or incredibly disturbing. Depends where you are on the scale of taking yourself too seriously or not taking yourself seriously enough. Personally, I swing wildly between the two, depending on if I've had my coffee yet.

Now, I bring this tiny mind-blowing fact up to lightly illustrate how a lot of us earth dwellers don't know who we really are. Sure, we have an identity. Our job, family, religion, net worth, sexual orientation, race, political affiliation, etc. But that's not who we really are.

Who we really are can't be taken from us. An identity can. When an identity is taken, our foundation gets rocked. Our false sense of self gone. Our false sense of purpose robbed. Our false sense of safety violated.

Thus, to avoid this inevitable falsity, I think one of the major goals in life is to drop the identity and find the Truth. The Truth of who and what we really are. Peel back the layers of the onion and see what's at the center. The part that is eternal. The part that is strength, fortitude, and love.

What is in there? Is it a flame? A soul? A higher self? God? A light? Maybe. Maybe it's all of it. Maybe it's none of it. Who knows.

But what I do know is that we are more than 60% Banana. And we are more than an identity. We are more than we think we are. So, let the adventure begin.

#3 Your Power Is Waiting

"Our deepest fear is not that we are inadequate. Our deepest fear is that we are powerful beyond measure. It is our light, not our darkness that most frightens us. We ask ourselves,

'Who am I to be brilliant, gorgeous, talented, fabulous?'

Actually, who are you not to be? You are a child of God. Your playing small does not serve the world. There is nothing enlightened about shrinking so that other people won't feel insecure around you. We are all meant to shine as children do. We were born to make manifest the glory of God that is within us. It's not just in some of us; it's in everyone. And as we let our own light shine, we unconsciously give other people permission to do the same. As we are liberated from our own fear, our presence automatically liberates others."

Marianne Williamson

I worked with a woman who was just beginning a second chapter of her life at 75 years old. We worked out of her gorgeous home in Brooklyn. When I was there, I was always struck by these huge paintings on her wall. They were stunning and vibrant. Nothing like I'd ever seen before. I asked her where she got them and she said that she painted them. All of them!

It turns out that she grew up in a small, very religious village in Haiti where women weren't allowed to paint with color. It was a sin. If they painted they were considered whores, unmarriable, and punishable by their local magistrate. So, she didn't paint.

Fast forward 20 years and one night in her home, she awoke in a cold sweat. Strange thoughts swirled through her mind. She saw colors. Images. They were obscene in their beauty. She had to paint! She had to paint with all the colors! And so she did. She painted on anything she could. It was a purge of the oppression from her childhood. The vitriol that had been cast upon her. Ohh, but it was also a reconnection. A reconnection to something that had been lost.

A flame had been re-ignited. Sometimes she would paint for 24-hours straight. Never stopping. She said God had given her permission to paint and all of it just flowed out of her. She was open! She was feeling her power.

She told me that we can either be free from our past or prisoners of it. That night, when she began painting again, she was finally free.

Most of us have experienced marked periods in our lives where we were made to shut our power down. Where we were forced to hide and repress it because of judgment. However, no more. Whatever part inside you that was deemed unworthy, let it rise. Let it live. It is your power. It is your life. It took this woman decades to rediscover hers, but she did. Her power was her color. What's yours?

#4 Lean Into The Revolution

"The most important kind of freedom is to be what you really are. You trade in your reality for a role. You trade in your sense for an act. You give up your ability to feel, and in exchange, put on a mask. There can't be any large-scale revolution until there's a personal revolution, on an individual level. It's got to happen inside first."

Jim Morrison

There are some immutable facts in life. We know that we are 60% Banana. We know that no one is making it out of here alive. We know we each have a choice in every situation. We know we are more than we think we are.

And…we know change is inevitable. The Greek philosopher Heraclitus put it best, *"There is nothing permanent except change."*

Thus, we too will change. We will have a revolution of the Self.

When the revolution comes, in whatever form, it is best to embrace it, not resist it. Again, it is inevitable.

When we resist, we suffer. We are pulled into a tornado of chaos and become the victim of it.

Or we can lean into this change. This revolution. We can acknowledge it. Feel it. Own it. Open to it.

Will it hurt? Maybe.

Will you need to let go of control? Possibly.

But once you do, you can ride it. Like surfing a wave. On top of it as opposed to in the churn.

The revolution occurs as a way to grow. To step outside of limitations. To become more. When looked at from that perspective, it may even be...fun.

Surrender to the revolution and go further than ever thought imaginable.

#5 No Permission Needed...

"But it's a poor fellow who can't take his pleasure without asking other people's permission."

Herman Hesse

I have a friend who is constantly reminding me that I can do whatever I want. "Whatever I want!" "But, but, but, but, won't I be irresponsible, won't I be broke, won't I be lazy and worthless?" These thoughts pour through my head. I mean, I have been somewhat of a follower throughout my life. I lived through the paths forged by others. The well-behaved school boy deeply embedded in my psyche.

But, there is another part of me that rebels against constraints. It loathes conformity. And it acts out. It used to like to blow up my life so it could begin anew. Ah, the good ol' days. No more blowing up. Instead, ownership. Ownership of every facet of my life. Time, feelings, the good, the bad, and the ugly. It's like I had to grant myself permission to be me first before I could start living.

So, while you do not need my permission, I am going to give it to you anyway.

Permission:

To be yourself.

To be jealous. To be afraid. To be gluttonous. To be lazy.

To be madly in love. To fall out of love. To laugh at inappropriate moments.

To be sick. To explore. To never get it right. To sweat. To have hair on your back.

To love your body. To forget to pay rent. To cry at insurance commercials.

To want the divine. To curse the divine.

To rear end a car. To rear end your partner.

To feel unworthy. To fear your own power. To love your own power.

To drink too much. To hurt someone you love. To be hurt by someone you love.

To feel powerful one day and nothing the next.

To love 80's music and loathe jazz. And the reverse.

To have no fucking clue what you are doing.

To love the world and hate it all in one breath.

To be you. To be human.

To be it all.

Permission Granted.

#6 It's All On Loan

"Remember that all we have is 'on loan' from Fortune, which can reclaim it without our permission—indeed, without even advance notice. Thus, we should love all our dear ones, but always with the thought that we have no promise that we may keep them forever—nay, no promise even that we may keep them for long."

Seneca

It's all on loan.

Our bodies, minds, homes, families, partners, jobs, cars, and our cats…

It's like a kid building with blocks. She can build huge castles. Forts. Bridges. Cities. All HERS.

But, at some point, they will have to be taken down. Cleaned up. And put away to be created into another fantasy for another day.

Kind of like life.

To know it's all on loan is both confronting and freeing. It wakes up! It removes the burden of needing "more."

It is your ticket to liberation.

#7 Ask

"Life's not about feeling better, it's about getting the job done."

Ned Vizzini

In the early years of my business, I almost missed out on one of my biggest corporate contracts because I didn't ask.

A few years ago, after finishing up a feng shui workshop I gave at Boston Consulting Group, I overheard someone mention in passing that it may be interesting for me to come back and do one-to-one coaching. My ears perked up immediately. I thought that could be an interesting way to engage the employees.

A few weeks went by and I hadn't thought anything of it. Then I saw the show *Billions* on T.V. and lo and behold there was this character, Wendy Rhoades. A corporate coach for a hedge fund. She was passionate, fierce, and really knew how to speak to people in stressful, high pressure situations. I loved it. That's what I wanted to do! But how?

I thought it was a ridiculous notion that BCG would want lil ol' me to coach their top consultants. But, I still asked. And then I put it out of my mind.

A few weeks went by and I got a call from the events manager. It turned out they did want lil ol' me. And it turned out that I would become their in-house coach for several years. Incredible.

If I had pooh-poohed the idea that I could be Wendy Rhoades or totally disregarded the offhanded comment that I could potentially coach one-to-one, I would not be here. I would never have pushed myself to a new level. I never would have known just how big of an impact I could make.

But I asked, and they said yes.

It never hurts.

And as the great Maya Angelou said: "Ask for what you want and be prepared to get it!"

#8 It's Over When You Say It's Over

"Man may have discovered fire, but women discovered how to play with it."

Candace Bushnell

Warning: Strong language. Either cover your eyes, have a lawyer redact the offensive words, or simply replace the bad words with "giggle." Ex: I "fucking" love cats. Now: I "giggle" love cats.

Ok, let's begin.

I was listening to this P!nk song called "I Am Here," and there was a particular line that struck me as quite interesting. In this song she's claiming what she wants. She's telling the world. Nothing to hide. I loved it!

"I wanna make some mistakes, I wanna sleep in the mud
I wanna swim in the flood, I wanna fuck 'til I'm done
I like whiskey on ice, I like sun in my eyes
I wanna burn it all down, so let's start a fire
I wanna be lost, so lost that I'm found
Naked and laughing with my blood on the ground"

The line that struck me?

"I wanna fuck 'til I'm done."

Her demanding that sex ain't over until she's done!

"I wanna fuck 'til I'm done."

It got me asking, where are the places in our lives that we don't fuck 'til we're done?

Where are the places we settle for a half of a fuck? Or a quarter? Or none at all?

Where are the places we don't even know we are allowed to say "I wanna fuck 'til I'm done?"

Where is life one habituated, unconscious pattern of sleep?

Where is the wool pulled over our eyes and we don't even know we don't know that we don't know?

P!nk claimed her life. She claimed her time. Her space. Her body. Her importance.

So, if you want to be like P!nk, claim it. Own it.

And for the love of God, fuck 'til you're done!

#9 Sacrifice For Your Mission

"Life is a suicide mission."

Orson Scott Card

When I was an actor out in Los Angeles back in the early 2000's, I owned a Dodge Stratus. My mom gave me the family car to drive cross-country to pursue my dream of becoming an actor.

This car was my chariot. A king among kings. It was my ticket to Hollywood.

Slowly but surely, in the truest form of American automotive engineering, it started to fall apart. But it didn't stop me. I was on a mission.

One day I got a call from my talent manager, "You need to go to Spelling Studios and audition for the TV show *Charmed*." Done. This was my big break and nothing was going to stop me. NOTHING.

Ahh, but alas, the Dodge Stratus had other plans.

As I drove down Miracle Mile, the engine started to overheat. Didn't care. I could throw water on it. I had ten minutes to make the audition.

Then smoke started billowing out. Didn't care!

Then fire. I cared.

I pulled over right outside the building where my audition was held, flung open the hood, and WOOF, flames. Everywhere. I HAD NO TIME FOR THIS. My entire future depended on it.

Water didn't work. I didn't know what to do. Time was ticking. Did I deal with the car a' flamin' or go to the audition? My chariot. My ticket. My baby. Sophie's choice.

I let it burn.

I chose the audition.

I went out there to act. I went out there to succeed. I went out there for a dream. And I sure as fuck wasn't going to let a little flaming car stop me.

I got the role. I was on *Charmed*. I was also able to get into the Screen Actors Guild and my dad covered the fees so I would have health insurance! Big breaks for me.

And the car? Burnt to a crisp. Plus, the good ol' LAPD found it necessary to give me a parking ticket for my flaming car. Classic.

So, here's the thing. There is always a flaming car. There will always be a flaming car. Where there is a dream, there will be a flaming car. It will test you. There will be rules. Rules that "shouldn't" be broken.

The shoulds, needs, have tos. So many good reasons not to break the rules.

It's not always easy to pass by a flaming car, but if we know it's going to be there, then at least we can bring a fire extinguisher and move on.

Let nothing interrupt the mission. The dream. Not the Rules. And certainly not a little flaming car.

#10 Success Don't Give A Fuck About "Rules"

"Rules? PISS ON YOUR FUCKING RULES!"

Ken Kesey

There's a little pizza place in Coney Island, NY called Totonno's. There, they don't give a fuck about the "rules."

They defy what the rules are for a "successful" restaurant.

A line around the door. It will take at least 60 minutes to get your order.

They're snarky. They've been around for 93 years. They have a right to be.

They don't need me. They don't care about Instagram. They aren't going to call you when your table is ready. You can get your water out of the same sink you wash your hands in.

It's the pizza they care about. And you can taste it.
The crust is like being transported back in time. It's rustic.
It's family. It's old school. It's Italy.

Order by the slice? Don't you even dare.

This pizza is meant to be eaten whole. Hot. Fresh. Anything less would be a disgrace.

A two-hour wait? On a light day!

Maybe, just maybe, the love of the craft and the art of creation still stands for itself.

In a world of cheap, fast, processed...Totonno's genuine, slow, fresh is what sells.

Maybe not giving a fuck about the rules is the rule. Maybe.

#11 Be The Leader In Your Life

"Everyone has talent. What's rare is the courage to follow it to the dark places where it leads."

Erica Jong

Remember, you are the leader of your life. No one else.

It is not your thoughts. Fears. Emotions. Unknowns.

It is not your boss. Your past. Your future. Time.

It is not your family. Cultural beliefs. Societal norms.

It is none of those things.

Those things can dictate how you live. How you make choices. They can hijack leadership.

But, we have sole ownership of our lives. No matter what. Nothing can take that away.

We must make our rules.

We must decide what is right for us and what is not.

We must choose who, what, where, when, why, and how.

It is time for us to all be the leader.

#12 You Have Beaten The Odds

"But I don't want to go among mad people," Alice remarked.
"Oh, you can't help that," said the Cat: "We're all mad here. I'm mad. You're mad."
"How do you know I'm mad?" said Alice.
"You must be," said the Cat, "or you wouldn't have come here."

Lewis Carroll

The odds of being born are 1 in 400 trillion. Let that sink in.

Factually, that means you are a winner. Something, somewhere won.

To be on this earth is something wild, it takes guts. It really does.

It's not for the weak. It takes a level of madness.

There is a certain level of stubbornness in us humans.

Some use that stubbornness to shut off the world and call it a day.

Others use it to forge ahead. Pushing through difficulties, large and small.

This stubbornness that forges ahead will accept nothing less than Truth.

It loathes falsity.

It takes guts because it is so easy to quit. To ignore decades of internal screaming.

But here we are. We are all here. Something inside us must want "this," whatever "this" is.

Somehow, we haven't quit.

And so, hats off to today.

Through all the hardships, the fuckups, the knockdowns, the victories, the abuses, the celebrations, the love, the darkness, the hate, the beauty, the destruction, the adventures, the you, the YOU!

We have made it to today. And on to the next.

#13 "I Refuse To" - Three Powerful Words

"It is one of the great joys of home ownership to fire a pistol in one's own bedroom."

Alfred Jarry

Me: What do you want to do to men?

Client: I want to fuck them up.

Me: Why?

Client: Because I refuse to be a victim to them anymore. They've been holding me back for years.

Me: Well, okay then.

She was one of my favorite clients. She hired me to help her find her balls again (her words, not mine). Somewhere in the midst of trying to navigate modernity she lost them. She was tired of the politics in her office. Tired of trying to date and play the games. She was tired of trying to figure out what was acceptable and what was not.

She was just tired.

So, we decided that it was time that she refused to live that way anymore. And that was her mantra: I Refuse To. It was so simple and so powerful. Any time she was presented with a situation that she did not like, she said her mantra. It was like a laser cutting through the bullshit. There wasn't any analyzing. Any rationalizing. Anything. She either wanted to or did not.

And wouldn't you know, she got her balls back.

"I refuse to..."

Here are a few examples she used:

I refuse to be afraid.

I refuse to play small.

I refuse to hide.

I refuse to suffer.

I refuse to compromise.

I refuse to judge.

I refuse to take on your words as my own.

I refuse to bite my tongue.

I refuse to quiet my anger.

I refuse to kiss you on the first date.

I refuse to listen to your opinions.

I refuse to be here.

I refuse to…

The power was hers again.

#14 No Is A Yes

"Do not allow people to dim your shine because they are blinded. Tell them to put on some sunglasses, cuz we were born this way bitch!"

Lady Gaga

The joy of saying NO.

It's so small. So tiny. And yet, so powerful.

NO can mean there is a more important YES on the other side.

That the YES is worth fighting for.

That the YES is clear and concise. It is ownership. It is definitive.

While some see NO as a bad thing,

To me, NO is honoring the coveted YES.

And saying YES is damn beautiful.

#15 Hold The "LOL"

"If you want to be respected by others, the great thing is to respect yourself. Only by that, only by self-respect will you compel others to respect you."

Fyodor Dostoyevsky

A friend I've known for 20 plus years, once wrote me a text that was so deep and vulnerable that it made me cry. He was expressing gratitude for something that had meaning to him. It was the first time I had ever read anything like this from him. Straight from the heart.

And then he ended it with a self-deprecating joke and an LOL.

Ugh. I get it. It went deep. That's hard to hold. It eases something to add an LOL.

It deflects the fear of humiliation.

The "LOL." The smiley face. The "hahaha." The self-deprecation.

I've been noticing in conversations, emails, and texts, that someone will say or write something very near and dear to their hearts, something with that vulnerability, and then— follow up with a laugh or an emoji.

And don't get me wrong, the reason I recognize it is because I'm guilty of it too. Lol. Haha. ;)

It's important to catch this.

This doesn't mean that you need to stop laughing. Stop being goofy. Stop having fun. Stop using LOL.

No, not at all. But own how you feel. If it's important, there is no reason to minimize it with a deflection mechanism.

Will it be easy to be that vulnerable? Depends. Will it be difficult to break that habit? Possibly. But...

Let's stop cheapening ourselves, our feelings, and our words.

Period!

#16 The Narrative Is Created By You

"My experience of life is that it is not divided up into genres; it's a horrifying, romantic, tragic, comical, science-fiction cowboy detective novel. You know, with a bit of pornography if you're lucky."

Alan Moore

I have lived in Greensburg, State College, Seville (Spain), Los Angeles, Philadelphia, Miami, Washington, D.C., Chicago, Dallas, and New York.

I have been a dishwasher, car washer, bagger, lifeguard, retail clerk, roofer, telemarketer, UPS deliverer, U.S. census taker, actor, talent manager, cocktail server, waiter, attorney, feng shui expert, Theta healer, life coach, IST practitioner, co-founder, and advisor.

I have had phenomenal relationships. I have had disastrous relationships.

I have failed more than I have succeeded.

And for many years, I felt like a failure. That was my narrative. Failure. I would think of everything I had done in life and chastise myself for it all.

However, after some serious work on myself, I was able to take a step back and pause. Pause the self-hate. Pause the narrative. Pause the bullshit.

And that's when I consciously chose my narrative. I didn't let it choose me. I mean, fuck, it's my life. No one else should choose your narrative. NO ONE!

See, this life is an experiment. A wild, ever-changing, bucking bronco of an experiment. And when I look back at where I've lived and what I've done, I have to smile. What an incredible ride. It has not been easy.

But my god, what an experiment.

And that's my new narrative: It's all an experiment. There is nothing fixed. Nothing! It will not last. There is no right way to do it. So when you look at your life, how will you look at it?

As a stunning experiment?

I hope so. And one with a bit of pornography, if you're lucky.

#17 Messiness Is Freeing

"I fear being like everyone I hate, I fear failure, I fear losing control. I love balancing between chaos and control with everything I do. I always have a fear of going one way or another, getting lost in something, or losing everything to get lost in. And I fear being a completely acceptable sheep in society."

Marilyn Manson

This comes from a blogpost I wrote one night a few years ago. I just couldn't get it out. I was stuck. Nothing was moving. And then, I remembered I could write whatever I wanted to. It was my damn blog after all. So, I just let this messy disaster flow. Here it is in the original form. Here's to the imperfect:

July 19, 2018
It's 11:12pm est. I'm writing it.

I'll be honest, I'm having writer's block. So let me share with you a free form stream of my consciousness to help me unblock this. I mean, I am human. So fuck it.

Feel free to stop reading and move to the next post. If you haven't moved on already, here we go:

I can't think. I can't think. my mind is racing. sugar is my god. I love Time After Time by Cyndi Lauper, Im listening to it now, I never listen to music when I write but I thought i would give it a try, it's not good. The music is but it messes with my brain. I ate a hot dog today with pizza and green tea ice cream followed by a diet coke, iced coffee and some peanut butter chumper things, I washed 4 loads of laundry with just oxy clean and found out that I was supposed to add detergent to it and now it smells like moth balls, that pissed me off. laundry is ridiculous. RIFUCKINGDICULOUS. I can't get the green tea ice cream out of my mouth, it was a pint, not proud. I love the boxers I'm wearing. Now george michael is playing. he did it right. I hate my apartment and love it at the same time. I want exposed brick. I have a decision to make but my mind is clouded and torn. I rode a rollercoaster today. It was fun but felt like it was crushing my brain. New york is a whore...sometimes. Lawyer, firemeow, green tea ice cream, probably lose a few followers, pout, rage, yell, manic, will i post this or delete it? blah blah blahalabhab blahbahla I almond butter. If I everrr say namaste in this blog and mean it, shoot me. fuckity fuck fuckerson fuckumps mrfuckertillywink sirfuckington assfuckcatdog ppoop. #Namaste

#18 Don't Be Precious

"Do you want to know who you are? Don't ask. Act! Action will delineate and define you."

Thomas Jefferson

Just write.
Don't edit.

These are the brilliant words my friend told me every time I got stuck in my writing process. It's what saved this book from being lost to oblivion.

I'd get stuck like any other person and I'd go to her to bail me out. However, the advice never changed.

Just write.
Don't edit.

These words, while brilliant, are maddeningly simple. Too simple, if you ask me! Ha. What about me needing to get the perfect laptop? The perfect chair? The perfect pen, outfit, mindset, weather, tea, book cover, meditation, inspiration...What about any other host of excuses I can throw at her?

Just write.
Don't edit.

This is applicable to life. Just do it. Don't stop. You don't need to be perfect. You don't have to be fully ready. You don't have to be confident. You will get stuck, disheartened, bored, but with those words as a north star, it is easy to march forward.

At the end of the day, almost every great success story comes down to just four words:

Just write.
Don't edit.

#19 Better To Find Joy Within

"The essence of philosophy is that a man should so live that his happiness shall depend as little as possible on external things."

Epictetus

The dependence on external factors to be joyous is dangerous. It is in dependence where we start to give our freedom away. Because dependence works two ways. If we have the thing we are depending on, great, we feel joy. But if we don't have it, bad, we feel no joy. It's just like being addicted to a drug. On it, we feel great. Not on it, we feel awful.

External-based joy is no different.

I am not saying don't experience joy when something good happens. Rather, start noticing when you're waiting for an event to change your mood and life. Again, if that external factor can bring you up, it can also bring you down.

Better to find joy within. Regardless of the circumstances. Regardless of the criteria. Regardless of the outside. If you get to that, you are living on a whole different level. One that is empowered. One that is fearless. Why? Because you rely on nothing but your internal being. Your force.

#20 Magic Is More Real Than "Real"

The Mad Hatter

Magic. I truly believe that deep down inside us, we all believe in magic. There is something profoundly real inside us that believes. Or better yet, something that knows. That knows something is much more than the material world. That is stunningly beautiful. This is why I included this article. It is magic.

In 1897, a young girl wrote to *The Sun*, a New York newspaper, asking if there was a Santa Claus. Here is the response:

"We take pleasure in answering thus prominently the communication below, expressing at the same time our great gratification that its faithful author is numbered among the friends of The Sun:

Dear Editor—

I am 8 years old. Some of my little friends say there is no Santa Claus. Papa says, "If you see it in The Sun, it's so." Please tell me the truth, is there a Santa Claus?

Virginia O'Hanlon
115 West Ninety Fifth Street

Virginia, your little friends are wrong. They have been affected by the skepticism of a skeptical age. They do not believe except they see. They think that nothing can be which is not comprehensible by their little minds. All minds, Virginia, whether they be men's or children's, are little. In this great universe of ours, man is a mere insect, an ant, in his intellect as compared with the boundless world about him, as measured by the intelligence capable of grasping the whole of truth and knowledge.

Yes, Virginia, there is a Santa Claus. He exists as certainly as love and generosity and devotion exist, and you know that they abound and give to your life its highest beauty and joy. Alas! how dreary would be the world if there were no Santa Claus! It would be as dreary as if there were no Virginias.

There would be no childlike faith then, no poetry, no romance to make tolerable this existence.

We should have no enjoyment except in sense and sight. The external light with which childhood fills the world would be extinguished.

Not believe in Santa Claus! You might as well not believe in fairies. You might get your papa to hire men to watch in all the chimneys on Christmas Eve to catch Santa Claus, but even if you did not see Santa Claus coming down, what would that prove? Nobody sees Santa Claus, but that is no sign that there is no Santa Claus. The most real things in the world are those that neither children nor men can see. Did you ever see fairies dancing on the lawn? Of course not, but that's no proof that they are not there. Nobody can conceive or imagine all the wonders there are unseen and unseeable in the world.

You tear apart the baby's rattle and see what makes the noise inside, but there is a veil covering the unseen world which is not the strongest man, nor even the united strength of all the strongest men that ever lived could tear apart. Only faith, poetry, love, romance, can push aside that curtain and view and picture the supernal beauty and glory beyond. Is it all real? Ah, Virginia, in all this world there is nothing else real and abiding.

No Santa Claus! Thank God! He lives and lives forever. A thousand years from now, Virginia, nay 10 times 10,000 years from now, he will continue to make glad the heart of childhood."

"Is There a Santa Claus?" reprinted from the September 21, 1897, number of *The Sun*."

II. Your Choice

#21 We Have A Choice

"We are our choices."

Jean-Paul Sartre

It is essential to remember we always have a choice.

This choice, this free will, is what distinguishes us from the animals.

We have the capacity to choose our lives. Who and what we want to be. How we want to live.

This choice becomes us. We become our choices.

It is a commitment at a deep level to separate from those who don't choose. It is a commitment to oneself to think for oneself. It is a commitment to awaken through our choices.

It is a commitment to the soul.

Remember, we have a choice!

#22 If You Jump, JUMP!

"If we listened to our intellect we'd never have a love affair. We'd never have a friendship. We'd never go in business because we'd be cynical: 'It's gonna go wrong.' Or 'She's going to hurt me.' Or, 'I've had a couple of bad love affairs, so therefore . . .' Well, that's nonsense. You're going to miss life. You've got to jump off the cliff all the time and build your wings on the way down."

Ray Bradbury

Fall down. Get up. Fall down. This was what I literally did back when I was living in California, around 2003. At the time I was trying my hand at acting, just like everyone else in Los Angeles.

I was young, I had hair, the world was my oyster. One day, I was getting new headshots taken in a park and lo and behold, there was an audition going on. Normally you have to be invited to audition or go through your talent agent.

They HATE when people attempt to audition without being asked to. I did just that.

It was for the Mini Cooper Convertible. How could I not crash this audition? It was huge!

So, I walked up, made something up, told them they lost my information and that they needed to see me. They bought it for some reason and sent me to the area to begin. How hard could it be? Give me lines and I'll act something out. Boom, done.

It turns out, the reason they were being so strict with this audition was that they specifically needed highly skilled gymnasts. Professional damn gymnasts! Ones that could somersault in the air off a trampoline and land on two feet.

When I heard this, my stomach dropped. Oh fuck. Fuck. Fuck. Fuck.

I couldn't do that. I couldn't even successfully jump on a trampoline without falling off, let alone flip in the air and land it perfectly.

But, there I was. I had to go through with it. Especially since I got myself in this ridiculous predicament.

Each actor/gymnast got two attempts. Most landed it with ease. I mean, they were real gymnasts!

So, I go up and make some jokes, hoping I can get out of it. No chance. Then they push me and tell me to run, bounce, flip.

I run to the trampoline, jump as hard as I can, legs buckle, and smash my face off my knees. Bloody lip. Bruised ego. That was attempt one.

Attempt two went just a bit differently. Lip bleeding and clearly not a gymnast, more people had gathered to watch this trainwreck. They knew what I was. And so I ran, I jumped on that trampoline, and I hit it as hard as I could. Part fear, part rage. I launched into space. As I was returning to earth, I saw the safety pads...and overshot them. And instead chose a particularly rocky place to land face first. That one hurt. I just stayed there.

The casting agent walked up to me and said, "You crashed this, didn't you?" Blood, dirt, ego, I said, "Yes."

She picked me up, got me some ice, and said, "That was the stupidest thing you could have ever done. Now please leave."

I left.

I didn't get the part. There was no award for trying. I didn't end up meeting someone really cool.

But I did leave with this: I fucking gave it my all. And that was one thing I could be proud of.

I realize most of the time I've felt like a failure in this life was when I half-assed it. Didn't really try one way or another. But when I did try 100% and failed, it never felt like a failure. It felt like victory, because in the end there was nothing else I could do.

Each day can be like this. Each moment can be 100% all in.

That said, I still cringe when I see a convertible Mini Cooper.

#23 Commit - As If Your Life Depends On It

"Socrates had it wrong; it is not the unexamined but finally the uncommitted life that is not worth living."

William Sloane Coffin

On the night before my wedding, I was speaking to my father-in-law, who is an ex-FBI agent. I was talking about work, life, and the fear of making the wrong choices. I asked how he made his decisions, especially when people's lives were on the line.

And he said, "You choose. You just fucking choose. And then commit. Totally commit."

It made sense, in his line of work there was no room for ambiguity. People lived or died by his choice to commit.

I married his daughter the next day. And committed.

Not committing is a slow and painful death while living this grand experiment. Half-in, half-out. It's a safe way to live. Not too much commitment one way or the other. Not choosing. Hedging your bets. If one fails, you always have a backup.

That's fine. To a point. Until...it's not fine anymore.

Until you're not fully living. Fully engaged in the here and now. Fully aware of every choice.

But why don't we commit? Fear.

What if I fail? What if I'm not good enough? What if, what if, what if?

Those are fair questions. But the truth is, if you are half-in and half-out, you aren't fully living. It's a half-life.

So what do you do? Choose. It's simple but not easy. It can be brutal. But not choosing is how you die. Trust me—I lived a huge chunk of my life never choosing. Always living in this ambiguous grey area.

Maybe the real problem is that nowadays we aren't forced to choose. We can live a safe, complacent life, half-in, half-out. Well, what if your life depended on it? What if it did matter, right NOW?

What would you choose? Choose it. Then do it.

#24 Lean Into The Fear

"Don't be afraid of your fears. They're not there to scare you. They're there to let you know that something is worth it."

C. JoyBell C.

I was at an event, speaking to the head of a company about her relationship to fear. As it turned out, she is a very introverted, shy, and fearful person. These qualities made her job as a leader extremely difficult. She told me there came a point in her life where she knew she had a choice to make—continue running from the fear or lean into it.

She leaned into it.

In any situation that brought up fear, she simply paused, breathed, and faced it head on.

Why? Because she knew that on the other side of fear was courage. Power. Happiness.

She still feels the fear. The shyness. And yet when the fear comes, she knows it is a cue for growth.

Because she chooses to lean into the fear, she is wildly successful.

Use fear as a mechanism of transformation. Use it as your secret weapon. And get ready to discover what is on the other side of it.

#25 Complacency Is A Death Knell

"If there's anything more important than my ego around, I want it caught and shot now."

Douglas Adams

One day, I was sparring in my muay thai class, and something funny happened.

I went up against this guy who surprised the hell out of me. He was around 5'4, and I'm about 6'1. I'd seen him fight— he was incredibly serious and dedicated to the sport.

But when we got to this technique called clinching, he dominated me. See, in clinching, you hold pads at waist level so your opponent can practice jamming his knee into your gut with full force. The opponent wraps his gloves around your neck to bring you closer while he tries to break your ribs.

Well, normally you're partnered up with someone similar to your own height, so height is not normally an issue. When I was partnered up with mister 5'4, I was curious how it would play out. One could say I was even a little...cocky.

Turns out this sonofabitch was ruthless. He pulled me down to his level and just held me there while throwing knees. I tried to straighten my back and he just kept at it. It was a death grip. And he threw me across the room.

Besides gaining a few bruised ribs and a bruised ego, I realized something very important. He was out to win.

He had to figure out a way to level the playing field against tall guys like myself: pure brute strength, stamina, and determination. He HAD to figure it out, or he would lose.

I never had to. I was comfortable. Complacent. I could go in, kick and punch hard, and get out. Maybe get a coconut water when I was done.

I always say comfort is going to be the death of us all. And I got a taste. I had a messed-up shoulder, swollen foot, and ribs that spoke to me every time I sneezed. There was no one to blame but myself.

I take this reminder to Wake The Fuck Up. To enjoy the comfort, yes, but to also remember, it ain't gonna last. It can't. None of us are getting out alive. And as long as I go in with guns a blazin' instead of with an almond milk latte, I have a fighting chance.

#26 Can You Stomach It?

"If you're going to try, go all the way. Otherwise, don't even start. This could mean losing girlfriends, wives, relatives and maybe even your mind. It could mean not eating for three or four days. It could mean freezing on a park bench. It could mean jail. It could mean derision. It could mean mockery-- isolation. Isolation is the gift. All the others are a test of your endurance, of how much you really want to do it. And, you'll do it, despite rejection and the worst odds. And it will be better than anything else you can imagine. If you're going to try, go all the way. There is no other feeling like that. You will be alone with the gods, and the nights will flame with fire. You will ride life straight to perfect laughter. It's the only good fight there is."

Charles Bukowski

"Can you stomach it? Can you stomach working on something you hate for seven years knowing it's the thing you have to do? Can you become obsessed about it?" This is what Dakota Jackson, the famous modern American furniture designer once asked me. I had led him and his partner in a meditation at a retreat center in the Catskills.

After the meditation, we three began to talk about life, breaking limits, and forging through adversity.

He asked me again, "Can you stomach it? Can you fully stomach going all the way on a project? Life?" It's a question he said most people don't ask themselves before beginning something that really matters. He said the reason he is where he is today is because he didn't bullshit himself. He thought big. Very big. Some would say even unreasonably big. But he always asked himself if he could stomach it. What would that take? How far would he have to go? What would he have to give up? What part of himself would he have to face? What part would have to rise?

Looking at Dakota's work and reading about his life, you begin to realize he truly asked himself that question. Each and every project he created required a commitment beyond "normal" standards. It required true dedication.

And as he said to me, "If you can't stomach it, fine, walk away. No more time needed on it." We don't have to judge when we walk away, but we do need to be truthful with ourselves.

If there is a project, an idea, a path that you've always wanted to take, begin by first asking yourself, "Can you stomach it?" From there you will have set the foundation for success with total truth and transparency to yourself.

#27 Care Deeply In Life

"The best books come from someplace deep inside....Become emotionally involved. If you don't care about your characters, your readers won't either."

Judy Blume

As I sat down at the counter to order ramen noodles in Greenpoint, Brooklyn, I was hesitant to say the least. I still have PTSD from eating mass quantities of "ramen" in college. And now, here I was in a pop-up ramen shop in the middle of a Swedish-inspired coffee house. Oh, New York.

As I sat there, this guy placed beautifully-crafted chopsticks down beside me, arranging them to be perfectly vertical.

He then asked which of the two dishes I wanted: Chicken or Vegetarian? Chicken, of course.

We started up a conversation. He described to me the 10-12-hour slow cooking of the shio paitan, a chicken-based stock with fish flavoring. The variety of spices, most of which I've never heard of, and the timing of each. The delicate balance of waiting for the spice to properly open but not missing the window to merge with the others.

He described how he goes to a farm upstate to get his chickens, which are all free-range. Never caged. It's a longer drive than to the local grocery store, but the slices have to be perfect. That's the other thing, it's not an American-size helping of meat. It's four little pieces that are cut fresh in front of you, seasoned, and then pan-fried.

By now I was dying. My mouth was watering. I didn't care what it would taste like. It was the sheer attention to detail, the adoration of the ingredients, and the artist's touch of creating this one-of-a-kind bowl of ramen that I had fallen in love with.

After the scallions were added, the chicken gently laid on top of the noodles, and Japanese pepper dashed in, the final ingredient was brought out. A half of a hard-boiled egg that had been marinated in 16 spices for over 24 hours. An egg! It was soaked and dripping with flavor. I felt like I was cheating on every other meal I'd ever had.

Once he served it to me, I completely lost my mind. It was like I was being presented with a Picasso. It had taken well over 20 minutes to make and in New York, that is an eternity.

The first slurp was like taking a lover into my arms after being away at sea for 40 years and finally having the first embrace. This was mine. The exquisite dance of flavors and artistry was all mine.

And as I sat there eating it, I was truly amazed at how this person was so completely dedicated to a bowl of ramen. In my world, that wouldn't make sense. Who has time for that? We are all so busy.

Things to achieve. Success to conquer. Ladders to climb.

And yet, here was one of the greatest, most memorable successes I've ever seen, in the back of a coffee shop, me falling in love with each spoonful of ramen.

Makes you see what's possible if we all had our own version of ramen.

Something we cared about so deeply that we would be willing to defy societal norms for.

Maybe we could make our lives like that? A dedication to life.

#28 Unlearn To Learn

"May you fight your own battles and forge your own wings."

Rainbow Rowell

When I almost failed out of law school my first semester in Miami, I realized very quickly that something was seriously off.

Granted, we had three devastating hurricanes. Black mold infestation in the dorms. And a whole lot of partying...it was Miami.

But what I realized was that I had never learned how to study. I learned how to do it like other people. I learned their tried and true methods. I did it for years. Memorization. Highlighting. Repetition.

Yet it never worked.

So, I had to start all over. My very good friend and I locked ourselves in our room and we deconstructed studying. What worked, what didn't. What was a distraction and what wasn't. What was easy but ineffective. We had to unearth learning methods that had never been taught. Never been tried.

We eventually came to the conclusion that I was a visual learner. I never knew that. Almost three decades and I never knew that.

We ended up diagramming and creating incredible visuals of legal issues, cases, ideas, rules, laws. We didn't use any electronics. No highlighters. We had huge whiteboards to write on with stunning colors.

It took longer. Oh yes. It took forever. But once we found the secret to my learning, I was on fire.

My GPA went from 2.6 to 3.69.

This is no different in life. Some of us never figured out how WE were meant to live. What our way of studying for life is...we just follow.

If you feel like you are hovering around a 2.6, maybe it's time to take a step back and unlearn how to live. Sometimes it's the fastest way to actually learn how to live.

#29 Break Free From The Prison

"Can you remember who you were, before the world told you who you should be?"

Charles Bukowski

Through meditation, it has become apparent that I am not what I think I am. I am not my mind. When I start to separate that out, it is quite jarring. It's beautiful but jarring.

It's very similar to a prison cell. One that we can decorate nicely. One that we can show our friends. One that has achievements. Goals. Family. New ideas, new thoughts, new distractions. A lifetime moving things around and upgrading. But...it will always be a prison cell. Four walls, a ceiling, and a floor.

No matter how "big" you become in that cell, no matter how much you conquer in that cell, no matter what, it is a cell. Just like the mind.

The only solution is to get out of prison. To leave the cell. To see more.

Most of us don't even know we are in a cell. We don't even know the limitations of our thoughts and beliefs. We don't even know.

When I meditate, I quiet the prison and slip through its bars. I silently move through "my mind" to a bigger space. Something more vast. Something more real. Something that is accessible to all of us. It's just that we have forgotten.

We have forgotten we are not our minds. We are infinite.

There is nothing wrong with being in prison. It is only "wrong" when it is unconscious and we are not choosing it by our own free will.

Looking forward to meeting you beyond the walls.

"You are wrong if you think Joy emanates only or principally from human relationships. God has placed it all around us. It is in everything and anything we might experience. We just have to have the courage to turn against our habitual lifestyle and engage in unconventional living."

Jon Krakauer

#30 Own The Divine Beast

"(T)he test of a first-rate intelligence is the ability to hold two opposed ideas in the mind at the same time, and still retain the ability to function.
One should, for example, be able to see that things are hopeless and yet be determined to make them otherwise. This philosophy fitted on to my early adult life, when I saw the improbable, the implausible, often the 'impossible,' come true."

F. Scott Fitzgerald

We humans don't really make sense. We aren't quite animals. We aren't quite angels. We're stuck somewhere in the middle. We are walking paradoxes.

On the whole, we've been taught to be angels. The perfect beings. Never to sin. We have a soul, but if we don't behave, it will be damned to a fiery inferno. God watches us, waiting to punish.

Not the most welcoming way to exist.

It has permeated our culture. Been shoved down our throats. Be kind. Loving. Forgiving. Grateful. Respectful. Honorable. Obedient. Intelligent. Successful. Shame-free. Guilt-free. Thought-free.

Ah, but alas, there is the part of us that is the animal. And animals are ANIMALS. We share 98% of our genes with gorillas. 60% with bananas. There is no denying what we are. And animals are no angels. Animals Kill. Fight. Fuck. Ravage. Feast. They sleep where they want, shit where they want, take what they want, do what they want. A one-track mind focused on survival.

Again. Somewhere in the middle, we are there. The Divine Beast.

But once we begin to accept that we are part gorilla, part cosmic whatever, we are free!

We can have dark "dangerous" thoughts, while at the same time weep for a newborn baby that we are absolutely in love with. We can hate with a fury of a thousand burning suns and yet feel devastatingly sad and vulnerable. Even Cicero understood the human condition: "The greatest pleasures are only narrowly separated from disgust."

We are paradoxical beings. It's glorious. Life becomes much more fun, simple, and powerful once we start to see both sides. And when we see those sides, it doesn't mean we're going to the office tomorrow to impale our co-worker with a six-foot, hand-carved stake because we feel blood-curdling rage. But neither are we going to renounce all cravings of the flesh and become monks.

All it means is that we start to get to know who we are and what is under the hood of this human being on our journey to discover ourselves. It is vitally important. VITALLY. This is the first step. Owning our paradoxical nature. That in itself should bring some relief to this wild ride called life.

"Do I contradict myself? Very well, then, I contradict myself; I am large -- I contain multitudes."

Walt Whitman

#31 Embrace The Funk

"Now and then it's good to pause in our pursuit of happiness and just be happy."

Guillaume Apollinaire

A client of mine was a machine at work. He could accomplish the mission at hand—no matter the cost, even to himself. He was driven on a completely different level.

However, that drive was driving my client crazy. He wanted to perfect perfection. He wanted to accomplish the unaccomplishable. To check off every box on the proverbial to-do list of life. It was maddening. He was driving himself mad.

So we paused. And I told him to do the opposite. A screeching halt of nothingness. To literally take his day and flip it on its head, repeatedly for a week. Here is what he wrote back:

I also wanted to let you know- I've also been putting into practice just doing whatever I feel like. You know what? Honestly I feel FANTASTIC man.

It's been so freeing to throw out my super long to-do list and just be. I watched a LOT of Netflix over the weekend and ate tons of junk food. I spent hours and hours on Instagram. I played mindless games for hours on end and let an entire day go by without getting out of bed.

Around the middle of this week though I got bored of all that and realized what I really wanted was more human connection and to feel good every day. I've started setting up tons of calls with friends to stay connected with people and meditating/reading more.

Still trying to learn how to fight the urges to be "productive" and get stuff done, but I'm definitely getting closer to just doing what I want to do and feeling much lighter because of it.

Thanks again for all the advice and support man. I'm excited to see where this goes! Already feeling so much better just to have the weight off my shoulders to "be productive."

Sometimes the best advice to be productive is to be unproductive.

#32 Perfection Is Imperfect

"Comparison is the thief of joy."

Theodore Roosevelt

Different body types, eyes, hair color, plants, animals, tongues, smiles, love, fingerprints, blood types, cries, smells.

Different.

We are different. We are a mash-up of different experiences, cultures, beliefs, sexuality, races, religions. We are mutts.

I get it, to not compare is difficult. Especially when we have a society that has force-fed us to believe we need to!

Ah, but if we can pause for a second and look at ourselves. See ourselves. Dropping all comparisons. What would we see? What do you see?

Embracing the difference in you. Seeing it as a strength instead of a weakness. I can't tell you how many times I've worked with people to find their special something and it often comes from a part of themselves that they judge!

Their potential superpower has been shut down, shot down, repressed, and judged! Why? Because it was different. It didn't fit the mold.

If we can let go of comparison and see ourselves, truly, we will see someone way more beautiful, powerful, and magical than we could ever imagine.

Someone different.

#33 Age Is Just A Number

"When I was your age, television was called books."

William Goldman

I began learning how to skateboard when I was 39.

My niece learned how to ride a bike when she was 7.

We both were excited. We both were scared.

We both asked for help.

I felt like a kid again. She felt like an adult.

Age is irrelevant in the pursuit of something outside your comfort zone.

If we stop learning, if we stop falling, if we stop reaching...age will matter.

Because it's at that age, the cessation of growth, that we begin to die.

But when we don't stop, we live.

7, 39, 47, 68, 72, 86, 98...these numbers are just the beginning.

So, begin!

#34 You Are Always Sexy

"What can I say? I've never met a cupcake I didn't want to get to know better."

Jasinda Wilder

I used to lead a lot of mindfulness workshops at Lululemon in NYC. It was my place to experiment with new ideas. They were fantastic about always letting me do whatever I wanted to try next. We built a relationship that lasted for years. Fast forward to one day when I received an email from them asking me to participate in a photoshoot. Lulu was opening a new store and they wanted to have people from the community in their new ad campaign. Awesome! I was in.

I got to the set of the shoot and immediately I felt like a movie star. I had an assistant take me into the trailer where the talent would be trying on outfits to wear. I was expecting "ordinary" people like myself. No six packs. Possibly a little hair where there shouldn't be. Maybe a bit soft around the middle. You know…"normal."

The people there were not "normal." They were goddamn models! There were six packs. There was no hair. There was no softness. Toned, sculpted gods. I stood there stunned: a) because they were all in their underwear trying on clothes; and b) because I had to join them.

Now, I'm not uber body conscious, but as I slowly disrobed I could feel how different I was from them. This pasty-ass body needed covering, immediately! I started to understand what it was like to feel less than. I started to judge. I just wanted to hide. I wanted to get the fuck out of there, especially because we were going to be half-naked for most of the shoot.

Two models/Alvin Ailey dancers saw this and came over and started speaking to me. They were fantastic. There we were, just a whisper away from being naked, chatting. Sure their quads could have been sculpted from marble, but they didn't care and they made sure I knew it. They wanted me not to care.

As the day went on and my shyness and judgment faded away, I began to realize it was all in my head. They really didn't care. They had their own battles to deal with. By the time the shoot was over, we were all closer than I could have imagined. And I think part of that was because we were all exposed. There was nothing really hidden. We were front and center, owning whatever the hell God gave us.

The body is the body. It is a meatsack that we were dealt. All different shapes, sizes, and colors. It is not something to be judged or shamed. Instead it is something to be loved. To be appreciated and admired.

I almost missed out on a very beautiful day of bonding with my fellow models (yes, I am now a model!) because I judged myself. I almost missed out on seeing the truth of the humans in front of me: their minds, their hearts, their souls. The meatsack is not us. It can never be us.

Time for all of us to be the models in our own lives. And by the way, to hell with six packs.

#35 Surrender The Need To Suffer

"People have a hard time letting go of their suffering. Out of a fear of the unknown, they prefer suffering that is familiar."

Thich Nhat Hanh

When I began my acting training at the William Esper School in Manhattan, I had no idea what was in store for me. I was a lawyer at the time and I worked out a deal with my bosses to let me leave to take classes, twice a week. It was something I had always wanted to do.

As I started diving into the different characters I played, I realized how absolutely taxing it was emotionally. And I had to go back to work for another six to eight-hours. Brutal. It really messed with my mind. It wasn't just me; I saw it taking the same emotional toll on everyone in my class. It was the embodiment of the artist suffering for their craft.

Some of the characters we played were alcoholics, murderers, abuse victims, etc. Not the easiest thing to do, to say the least. And you had to find that emotionality somewhere deep within. Most of us, after days of digging into our souls, did find it, but then the problem was how to get rid of it. The feelings would last for days. It was awful. We were suffering.

And it was stupid.

This is when I decided suffering had to be stopped. If I was going to continue to act, it would not be from a tortured life. Slowly, I began to dissect the idea of suffering. Why we hold onto the feelings. Why we don't move on. What we actually gain from suffering. Where the unconscious choice was made to suffer.

While the acting school highlighted suffering, it brought a much deeper realization to the surface. I liked to suffer. To me it was a badge of honor. It was a sign that I had worked hard and earned it. Holding onto those emotions projected to the world that I had endured great difficulties and won!

Not the healthiest way to live. But what was on the other side of suffering? Flow. Ease. Joy. Abundance. Clarity. When I started to remove the old paradigm of suffering, it was like the sun rising above the clouds for the first time. I had nothing to do but feel the warmth on my face and smile.

I could still access deep parts of myself for acting, but it flowed through me like a river over rocks. It never stopped needlessly to dwell; it just kept moving forward. Always adapting, always purposeful.

Suffering is an addiction. It is stupid. It is stuckness. It is needless. And we have a choice to flow forward.

#36 A Mistake Is Honorable

"Now go and make interesting mistakes, make amazing mistakes, make glorious and fantastic mistakes. Break rules. Leave the world more interesting for your being here."

Neil Gaiman

As evidenced in this book, I am the type of person who learns from the pain of making many mistakes and failures. Many, many mistakes and failures. I find it quick and efficient. It makes its point and I can course-correct. This way of learning isn't without its side effects. The main one being pain. But pain is different from suffering. As Haruki Murakami states, *"Pain is inevitable. Suffering is optional."*

Suffering is living in the past. Pain is current.

When I was in high school, all my friends were on the track team. I was not. In fact, up until senior year, I was in the marching band. But my best friend convinced me the band was for losers and we needed to quit and join track. Made sense. Track seemed like an easy lateral move for someone with no history of athletic ability...it would fit perfectly. So, I picked the most obvious track event that required very little skill or athletic ability. The Pole Vault.

Let me tell you something about pole vaulting. It is one of the most complex sports that exists in track and field. You are attempting to run down a track at top speed, land a 17-foot pole in a box the size of a deck of cards while inverting yourself over another pole and landing safely on a pad. I played the saxophone. Poorly. Sometimes I marched in place if I could remember the steps. I was not a pole vaulter.

It was an utter failure which I'm sure you could have guessed. The last time I ever pole vaulted was during a track meet. I ran as fast as I could, planted the pole and began my inversion over the pole when something went incredibly wrong. I failed to invert and instead the velocity from the cockeyed jump shot me face-first into a pillar that was holding the horizontal hurdle pole. I then completely missed the safety pad and smashed into the ground. To this day I have a chip missing out of my front tooth from hitting that pole.

Here's the thing, I sucked at track. I knew that. Part of my tooth was missing. My lip was swollen. That was painful. Great, time to course-correct. Sure, my ego was as bruised as my face. But, I picked myself up, dusted myself off, laughed/cried, and tried something new. It wasn't the end of the world. Suffering normally comes from the idea that a mistake/failure defines us. Becomes our identity. It is nothing of the sort. It is an event that happened in the past. It is ripe for learning and growing. If you survive said mistake, you have an opportunity that most people will never get. The ones that were too afraid to try. To try to live. Teddy Roosevelt put it best:

"The credit belongs to the man who is actually in the arena, whose face is marred by dust and sweat and blood; who strives valiantly; who errs, who comes short again and again, because there is no effort without error and shortcoming; but who does actually strive to do the deeds; who knows great enthusiasms, the great devotions; who spends himself in a worthy cause; who at the best knows in the end the triumph of high achievement, and who at the worst, if he fails, at least fails while daring greatly, so that his place shall never be with those cold and timid souls who neither know victory nor defeat."

#37 You May Just Not Give A Shit

---

*"The fuckers. There, I feel better. God-damned human race.
There, I feel better."*

Charles Bukowski

A client of mine cared. Oh lord, how he cared. He was incredibly caring in everything he did. He cared about the whales, the environment, his ex, her family, his co-workers, and his bosses. He cared about what social media told him to care about. He cared about what the news told him to care about. And he was exhausted. He was a shell of a man. More like a doormat.

When we dug in, we discovered that he "cared" out of a sense of obligation. He felt that he "should" or "had" to. His Irish Catholic upbringing was front and center. At a deeper level he worried what it would mean if he didn't care. Who would he be? A masochistic sycophant? A monster? Only indulging in his every desire and wish? And as we peeled back the onion, we found out he actually didn't care. Not one bit. He just didn't give a damn about any of it. Some program inside him simply told him he needed to. But no more.

This was the first step to freedom.

Don't get me wrong, it was difficult for him to accept this part of himself. This "uncaring" part. But what came of it was a sense of self. He could drop the martyrdom of being everyone's go-to guy and start focusing on other things. He could stop spending energy on other people that meant nothing to him. He could stop the energetic waste. He could focus on himself.

Focus on things...he cared about. That truly mattered. To him.

We are programmed to think we need to care. But we don't actually have to. It may sound callous—it's not. We don't all have to care. Especially about the same things. It's exhausting pretending. Even to ourselves.

But at the end of the day, you may just not give a shit. And that's okay.

#38 No One Gets Out Alive

"Everybody has a plan until they get punched in the mouth."

Mike Tyson

C'est la vie. We are all going to die. It is inevitable.

I once had a laptop crack my skull open when it fell from a five-story building.

I was almost impaled by a stick through the eye.

I almost suffocated to death because I accidentally inhaled foam at a party and it removed all the oxygen from my lungs.

I was driving a car and lost control and did a 360 through two lanes of oncoming traffic.

I was left behind on a snorkeling dive for two hours and was ten feet away from a shark.

I fell out of a tree directly onto my head.

I've been robbed, fought with, threatened, and pepper sprayed.

You can say it's been a full life. And each one of those things could have killed me. But so can going to bed. So can disease, a hard sneeze, sex, sushi, a lover, love!

It really doesn't matter HOW it will happen. What matters is acknowledging that it WILL happen. It is said that fear of death is the root of all fears. Every fear stems from that.

If we can start to associate and get to know how we feel about death, maybe we wouldn't be afraid. Maybe anxiety and stress would fade. Maybe we would start to live differently. Think differently.

Maybe, life can truly begin to be embraced by the fact—no one gets out alive.

III. Your Truth

#39 Success Is The Warmest Place To Hide.

"Success is not final, failure is not fatal: it is the courage to continue that counts."

Winston S. Churchill

I watched a video of the actor Terry Crews speaking about his early childhood and how brutal it was. And it was brutal. In it he says, "My earliest memory is my father hitting my mother in the face as hard as he could. And I remember seeing her on the floor and then looking at him, this giant of a man who I thought, my god he says he loves her, what is he going to do to me? And all I could think was how I want to protect her. How I want to protect her. And how wrong it was. And I said I gotta get strong. I gotta get strength. So that I can protect her."

He went on to talk about how that abuse permeated his life as he got older. The fears. The patterns. The trauma. The outbursts.

He spoke of his success and how, for all of that "success," he was still hiding. He used his success to mask the pain. To keep pushing for more and more in order to never have to face that pain again.

That's when he realized that *success is the warmest place to hide.*

We all want that one thing. That one thing that will make us feel better. Is it love? A better job? More money? Time? Family?

We want that success in that one damn area. We pray for it. But it never seems to come.

And from what I've seen, this only magnifies the pain. We desperately run from our wounds, hoping success will fill in the gaps. That's the wild part. Success magnifies the gaps. It makes them even more evident.

These pains we have now. The wounds. They are here to be acknowledged. Felt. Healed. Not replaced or sidestepped.

To be successful and enjoy ALL OF IT, a level of opening to what is here now is the most successful thing we can do. Opening to the pain. The trauma. The abuse. We all have levels of it. And if we embrace it, and acknowledge it, and heal it, we will be successful.

That's success. Heal the wounds and become wildly successful…just like Terry Crews.

#40 Happiness Cannot Be Bought, Unfortunately

"While money can't buy happiness, it certainly lets you choose your own form of misery."

Groucho Marx

A friend of mine sells high-end jewelry in France. By high-end, I'm talking about a handmade tiara going for $2.5 million dollars. So, high-end.

His customers spend a million dollars without batting an eye. $100k on a pair of earrings to wear once. $50k on a watch just for show. Rubies and diamonds the size of my head! Well, I have a big head, so probably not that size, but you get the point.

What I found most interesting was when he said, "They are no different than you and me. They are just like us. There is no difference! They simply hide their misery in much more expensive ways. That's it."

He said that on the inside their insecurities were raging. Fears aplenty. Sadness and loneliness abounded. Impostor syndrome. Always wondering what the next thing would be that could fulfill them. Searching. Buying. Searching. Buying.

The money. The jewels. The cars. The homes. "Success" never worked. It never eased the pain of being human.

I have yet to find an example where a material object quenched the ache of being human.

Not that I haven't tried. I know. I know it's hopeless.

That's the damn joke about this life of materialism we live. We think and pray for that external thing to fill the void inside. But it won't. It can't. Why?

Because the external is not the internal. It will never be the internal. It can never be the internal. It is the square peg into the round hole.

But once we see, we can stop trying. We can start looking inward. And heck, who knows, maybe after we embrace it all, we can get that tiara and wear it like the fabulous people we are.

#41 You Don't Have To Earn Your Life

"No man has the right to dictate what other men should perceive, create or produce, but all should be encouraged to reveal themselves, their perceptions and emotions, and to build confidence in the creative spirit."

Ansel Adams

"I've Earned this vacation."

"I've Earned a day off."

"I've Earned this car."

Earning. What an interesting concept. It must be Earned. Because if it isn't, what happens?

You become lazy? Egotistical? Slothful? Greedy? Unappreciative...or so we are led to believe.

So, you work hard for it. Save up. Pinch pennies. EARN IT! Just like your family did before you and theirs before them. Blood, sweat, tears, and sacrifice.

However, I wonder, must it be Earned? As you read this, see if there is a reaction in your body.

What if it came simply? What if it came easily? What if it came from something you loved doing?

Wouldn't that be something.

And the funny thing is that I think we would still be appreciative. We would still contribute to society.

I think this idea of Earning is an ingrained belief that helps us feel worthy about receiving something we want and deserve. Like a dog who does the trick for a treat.

Does this mean you should quit your job and wait to receive blindly from the universe? No. It means that IF we are all waiting to enjoy life until it has been Earned, we are fucked.

Start to see the beliefs around Earning. See if it is tied to a level of suffering. We may all be making this life a lot harder than it has to be simply because our definition is outdated.

#42 It's All Make Believe

"The older I get, the more I realize no one has any idea what they are actually doing and everyone is just pretending."

Unknown

A lot of my clients always feel like they are all alone in this world. Alone in this world in their feelings.

In their failures. In their struggle.

They feel that they are the only ones fucking up.

That there is no one else, ever, making the same mistake. And they think they are terrible people for it.

And that breaks my heart. I've felt that way. I know the weight of that. It's heavy and isolating.

But, alas, we are not alone. We are all human. We are all making mistakes. We are all "failing." We are all "screwed up." We are all "imperfect." We are all "less than." We are all...fill in the blank.

No one has the answers. They can't! If they did, they would be God. And that would be something I think a few of us would notice.

Accept the fact that no one really has a clue what is going on. We have some hints. We have some ideas. But truly, who really knows?

Both comforting and disturbing...and hopefully somewhere in the middle: freeing.

#43 Never Sacrifice Your Core Values

"I started my life with a single absolute: that the world was mine to shape in the image of my highest values and never to be given up to a lesser standard, no matter how long or hard the struggle."

Ayn Rand

When I was clerking for the Department of Justice, we had this case where an international drug smuggler was incarcerated and was waiting to be tried.

My boss and I went to the courthouse to depose him and get his version of the story for the record.

The guy starts off by saying that he was a farmer and the drug cartel forced him into being a smuggler. They shot his brother. Held his son hostage and threatened to systematically kill everyone else in his family if he didn't smuggle drugs for them. He said he had no choice.

His story was verified and he was telling the truth.

My boss told me he was guilty and he broke the law. He did. That was true.

But what about his family? They'd probably be killed. According to the government, it wasn't our problem. I was dumbfounded.

All I could think was, what in the absolute fuck was happening here? If I were in that position, I would fly drugs around the world in order to save my family. No question.

When I went home I couldn't stop thinking about him. He'd probably be in jail for the rest of his life. He would most likely never see his family again...if they were still alive. This wasn't my kind of justice. This, to me, was wrong. The whole situation was wrong.

The more cases I worked, the more I saw how easy it was to see crimes as black or white. How easy it was to get jaded as bad or good. Guilty or not guilty. I get it, these attorneys only have so much bandwidth. They have a job to get done. But not me. I couldn't do it like they did. It was so much more than black or white.

After my clerkship I decided not to pursue a career with the Department of Justice. Not an easy decision.

Had I stayed, I would have become something that wasn't me. I would have become very cold. Mechanical. The people in front of me, just a job to do. That's just me, though. Not everyone is like this.

This is not a critique of the legal system or morality. It is not about right or wrong.

It is simply to show you how easily we can disappear into a life that is not our own. One that has promises of "greatness." One that requires personal compromises. Maybe of values. Maybe of time.

I was not meant to be in that position. I couldn't go against who I knew I really was.

The "I" always knows the Truth...

And nothing but the Truth.

#44 Life Is Not Mutually Exclusive

"I'm the one that's got to die when it's time for me to die, so let me live my life the way I want to."

Jimi Hendrix

Life can be very bifurcated. It's something I think about a lot.

We have our work lives. We have our personal lives. Maybe we have a hobby thrown in there as well.

But how often do they blend together? Should they blend together?

For me, I'm finding the more I blend them, the happier I am. When I can bring the depth of my meditation into my "work" life, I feel fulfilled. The mindfulness. The quiet. The presence. The intention. The heart.

It is only when I think these two worlds can't coexist that I start to feel off.

Since these aren't mutually exclusive, there are certain qualities in each part of your life that you can bring into every part. Warmth, inspiration, humor, creativity, joy, love, etc. Those don't have to die the moment you transition to another part.

If you are finding one part of life to be lacking something from another, I recommend distilling the qualities out of the part that isn't. Figure out what those are and then bring them to the part that is lacking. Merge the two. Let it be a fluid, fulfilling life.

Soon, life will be a seamless joy of curiosity and connectedness.

#45 Ask For Help. Even When It's Hard.

"There's really no honor in proving that you can carry the entire load on your own shoulders. And...it's lonely."

Amanda Palmer

Life requires asking for help.

This is extremely important if we are going to be human.

Help requires an army. It requires the right people. The right moments. The right time.

Help requires a single action. It requires letting the word escape from your mouth.

Help requires vulnerability. It requires humility. It requires necessity.

Help requires boldness. It is not for the faint of heart.

Help changes lives. It shatters the past and begins anew.

HELP. Four letters that few have the courage to weave together. Maybe they've forgotten. Maybe they've never tried it. Maybe they're too afraid.

No matter. Help will come regardless of how loud or how soft. How timid or weak. How brash or brazen. It will come. And it will help.

#46 Every Second Matters

"Time is the coin of your life. You spend it. Do not allow others to spend it for you."

Carl Sandburg

Tim Urban, the author of the popular blog, *Wait But Why*, created a "Your Life in Weeks" calendar. It is essentially that, a calendar that shows a 90-year life in weeks. You input your current age and it greys out all the weeks you have lived up until that point. It shows you what you have left. What you have left...in a visual representation.

It is humbling.

Time is ours. We have an allotted amount. What we choose to do with it is up to us. No one else. We don't know how much we each have. But, when you see it broken down into potential weeks, the time remaining is much less than you think.

It becomes much more valuable.

It may encourage you to embrace it. Face it. Lean into it.

Each second may count more. Each minute. Each day. Each week.

Time is precious. Let yourself dream bigger. Let yourself act bolder. Let yourself love harder.

Tony Robbins has a great quote about time:

"Most people overestimate what they can do in a year and they underestimate what they can do in two or three decades."

Use it all up! Time to own our time.

#47 Consciously Choose

"On the day of my judgment, when I stand before God, and He asks me why did I kill one of his true miracles, what am I gonna say? That it was my job? My job?"

Stephen King, The Green Mile

Remember to live for more than the perks.

My neighbor and I were talking one day about jobs and the current corporate climate. He told me that he caught himself living for the perks. The lunches. The coffee. The meditations. The healthcare, etc.

Living for the perks. I had never heard of that. But wow, it made a lot of sense.

But, the perks cost something. He was slowly giving up his freedom. He left the office later. He compromised on things that were once important to him. Every time the job asked more, he noticed another perk. And he gave in to it.

As his freedom diminished, the perks increased. Not that this is a bad thing if you consciously choose the perks and realize what you are potentially sacrificing.

However, what scared him most was that he was unconscious of it all. He didn't see it coming. The manipulation. The loss of freedom. The longer hours. The bigger teams. More meetings. More weekends. MORE!

All he cared about was getting the next perk. It was the eternal carrot dangling in front of his nose.

Moral of the story? Awareness and choice.

It's not that one thing is bad or good. It is simply being aware and choosing consciously.

If you're going to give up your freedom, do it consciously.

And maybe for more than just a free latte.

#48 You Know What Is Right

"The trouble with being in the rat race is that even if you win, you're still a rat."

Lily Tomlin

A client once asked me, "Is there anything wrong with me if I'm not as stressed as my colleagues and not playing their games?"

His colleagues stay up until midnight and wake up at 6am. Working. Checking email. Responding. Always on. Always ready. Always willing to put the company above all. "Yes Men and Women." In essence, their identity was the company.

He felt like he wasn't doing something right. How would he be seen by others? Was he not as driven? Was he not playing the games correctly? Was success defined as always being available?

As we dug deeper, it was clear the answer was no. Nothing was wrong. In fact, this person was right. How do we know? Well, factually, this person has consistently scored higher in his reviews than anyone on his team. His work had been exemplary. But more importantly he was self-aware enough to question the system. To follow his intuition.

While it may seem obvious that he was doing something right, it begs a look into company culture and its deep influence on the psyche.

Here is someone who had an outstanding work product. He valued his time. He didn't fall victim to the games. He got enough sleep. He saw his family. He was successful.

So, why is this fear so pervasive? It erodes the foundation of confidence. Whispers in our sleep.

Company culture.

Culture is pervasive. It can be uplifting or insidious. It has its positives and its negatives. I'm all for an empowering company culture. But there are caveats.

The more we can separate ourselves from a culture, the stronger we become. The clearer we think. The more in control we feel. Even the good ones. We can end up enjoying the culture. It is important to have this separation so when we do engage with it, it is from a conscious space. An active decision rather than a reactive one. Not simply "following the leader."

#49 Simplicity Wins

"Somewhere, right at the bottom of one's own being, one generally does know where one should go and what one should do. But there are times when the clown we call 'I' behaves in such a distracting fashion that the inner voice cannot make its presence felt."

Carl Jung

Investor Anton Kreil states that in order to truly be successful, you must ditch the smartphone. Get a flip phone instead. He says this is non-negotiable.

The smartphone has removed all boundaries from people's lives. We no longer have time to exist. We don't have time to be creative, to find space, to push hard at the things that matter. He credits his flip phone as one of the core reasons he is as wildly successful as he is today.

It's an interesting argument. I can tell you that most of my clients who have incredibly intense jobs are all finding the erosion of their boundaries.

A 24/7 bombardment of emails, news, photos, texts, chats, opinions. Squeezed out of their own lives.
And so with all of these external forces piling on, what happens? A feeling of overwhelm. All of the time.

Why? Because we don't know who we are anymore. We don't know what we feel. What our problems are.

What are we avoiding? Are we growing? Are we challenging ourselves? Or are we simply coping?

So what do we do?

It's simple—find simplicity. We have to simplify the ever-living shit out of our lives.

Maybe that's a flip phone. Maybe it's less T.V. Maybe it's shutting it all off at a certain time. Maybe it's saying "No" more. Maybe it's deciding what is important in life.

We don't have a lot of time. But we do have a choice. A choice to simplify. A choice to live for the things that matter.

Time to learn how to use T9 texting again.

"It is not a daily increase, but a daily decrease. Hack away at the inessentials."

Bruce Lee

#50 Silence The Noise. Repeat.

"Never miss a good chance to shut up."

Will Rogers

I can't tell you the number of bad choices I've made from the noise in my head. A reactive, impetuous, bullheaded noise. I know the noise in my head well. It's loud. A lot of opinions. Chaotic. It likes shiny objects. It doesn't have time to feel shit. It likes things quick and easy. It has a cheap feel to it. The reward, immediate. The consequences, forever.

The noise. It's pollution to us human beings. A bombardment of interruptions.

And underneath that noise?

Silence.

And in that silence?

Presence.

And that presence is where clarity comes from. It is where I can see 360 degrees. Not just from the reactivity or shiny lights. It's where there is depth. Certitude. Non-reactiveness. Love.

Cultivating the silence in life is a phenomenal tool that too many of us ignore.

When the world gets too loud or WE get too loud, start looking for ways to quiet the noise.

It is in that quiet that you can find peace. You can find you. You can find Truth.

#51 Small Steps Leads To Big Success

"The journey of a thousand miles begins with a single step."

Lao Tzu

When I was an actor, my acting teacher would assign us parts. In these parts we would have to develop the character. Find his mannerisms. His speech. His thoughts. On top of that, we would have to find his words. Memorize them. Know them. Become them.

This made my brain shut down. Memorizing was my Achilles heel. I was never good at it. I didn't plan on being good at it. That said, it needed to be done.

So, he had us do this exercise: he made us calculate how long it would take to embody this character, memorization and all. What was the TOTAL time? Once we had the time, say 25 hours, we then calculated how long before our next class. Say, 14 days. We would then take the number of hours in the day that were actually available and began to piece out a schedule .

Some days we could only fit 30 minutes. Others 4 hours. It didn't matter, as long as we got that 25 hours in. The goal, no matter the size, was to get the time in.

What was so beautiful about breaking any "enormous" task down to the smallest doable unit was that it became possible.

Sure, I could find 15 minutes here. 2 hours there. No problem finding 45 minutes and then 1.5 hours. It became manageable.

Even today, if I don't break big tasks down but rather only focus on the total, I will fail. I will not start. But if I break it into manageable chunks, I become a success.

If there is a place in life that is stuck, use this method. The tiny steps to success will help change everything.

#52 If It Works, Make It A Habit

"We are what we repeatedly do. Excellence, then, is not an act, but a habit."

William Durant

Working out. Oh mama. How I loathe thee. Decades of starts and stops. Never quite finding that rhythm to endure.

When I turned 40 I swore I would not enter this decade fucking around anymore. I would get this body in shape once and for all. I hired a fitness coach and told him to annihilate me. Cut the fat off with a butcher knife if need be. Feed me rice and water in a prison cell! I was ready. But he had something else in mind.

Our first session: "Give me three pull-ups."
Me, "Three? I mean I can do that but ok."
Him, "Yeah, three." I did three pull-ups.
Then he said, "Do it again." I did it again.
We went on talking diet and other things and he said, "Hey can you do three more?"

This went on for 45 minutes. By the time it was done I had done 50 pull-ups. I had never done 50 pull-ups before. The next session he had me do the same thing with push-ups, sets of ten. I did 250 push-ups in 45 minutes. I had never done that either.

That was our workout. Nothing more. Nothing less. He just kept having me do three pull-ups, ten push-ups. He said to do it until it became a habit. Focus on nothing but that. It was so painfully simple. I did it until it became a habit. Since then we have added other exercises but the foundation never changes. Decades of shitty workouts whittled down to three and ten.

In developing said habit, we are not looking for results. We are not comparing. We are not analyzing. We are simply doing the thing over, and over, and over again. Showing up every single time.

Here are some keys to helping a habit stick:

1. Make it small. Do it in the most easily attainable time and size. Working out? 20 minutes? 15 minutes? Four times a week? Three? Whatever is actually doable, do that. And repeat.

2. Want it. Actually want to do it. Don't do it because you hate something about yourself. Do it because you want to grow. Because you want to change.

3. Fight for it. The day you want to quit is the day you must continue on. THAT IS THE MOST CRUCIAL DAY. The one day where you have rationalized every conceivable reason not to do it, do it then. You will break through massive resistance that will pay off in the long run.

Build the habit. Build your life. (Oh, I like that).

#53 How You Do Anything Is How You Do Everything

"I hate the indifferent. I believe that living means taking sides. Those who really live cannot help being a citizen and a partisan. Indifference and apathy are parasitism, perversion, not life. That is why I hate the indifferent."

Antonio Gramsci

I took an "Active Shooter" workshop in my Krav Maga martial arts class.

It was intense, to say the least.

There were two main goals of this class. #1. See how you instinctually react to someone shooting in close proximity. #2. React in an appropriate manner.

The appropriate reaction in an active shooter situation is run, hide, or fight. Only three options. And whatever you do, do it full out.

Depending on the proximity of the shooter, you choose one of those three things.

Putting this into action, something struck me in a way that I wasn't planning.

During the workshop, the instructor wanted us to treat it as if it were REAL. Mentally and physically. No half-assing it. Completely real.

At one point, a gun came out, and out of the three options, hiding seemed the best. So, I hid with a bunch of other people. It was the "right" thing to do. However, we were "wrong."

The teacher came to our hiding spot and asked us why we didn't go down the stairs. Why we didn't use the elevator next to us. Why we didn't grab any objects to defend ourselves. Why we didn't call 911. Why?!

Our answer? "It was a workshop." "It wasn't real." "We weren't thinking."

His answer? "Then you're dead."

Why? He said that by going half-assed, not going 100%, not going full on, life or death, even in this class, we were systematically training our bodies and mind to give up. To not fight for our lives. To react in the same passive way when and if it really did happen.

For him, there was no middle ground. It was life or death.
And either we train ourselves now or we wait to die.
How we do anything is how we do everything.

It hit home. Shook me a bit. And I started asking myself where do I show up like this in other areas of life?

Where I wait for the "training" to be over. Where I wait for it to be "real."

It revealed a lot. It's something worth reflecting on in life. Maybe you give it 100%, maybe you don't.

But waiting will lead to death. That is certain.

#54 Speak The Truth

"The truth does not change according to our ability to stomach it."

Flannery O'Connor

When I worked for the Chairman of the Senate Judiciary Committee, I had several bosses that made an impact on me. One helped me transfer law schools. Another helped me dive deep into how we were key to providing funding to different federal agencies. But one boss really stuck out. He was the chief counsel of the committee. He didn't say much and was the most seasoned in the office. Needless to say, I didn't have a lot of interaction with him.

One day we were working late at night on a bill that would go to the floor of Congress the next day. My job was to research legal precedent and make sure we weren't breaking any laws with this bill. It was about 10pm and there were only a few of us left in the office. I looked up to see my boss walking towards me and sit down at my desk.

He said, "Kennedy, right? That's your name?" I nodded. He looked at me and asked me if I knew why this work was important. I said that we wanted the bill to pass and not break the law. He looked at me and said that that was correct but it was more than that. He said it was truth. We owed the citizens of this country the truth. The truth of what the bill was. Of what the laws were. We owed them truth. "Truth matters, Kennedy."

And then he got up and left.

It always stuck with me. Here was a man who embodied what he said. He seemed to only speak the truth. Who honored the truth. And to whom truth mattered. It made me want to do the same.

Truth isn't easy. It's not always celebrated. But truth is freedom. And freedom is truth.

#55 Obedience Is Lame

"Disobedience is the true foundation of liberty. The obedient must be slaves."

Henry David Thoreau

So, what are the rules?

The rules of life, what are they?

We have morals, social norms, pacts, good faith promises, beliefs, systems. But are the rules? Who created them? Why were they created? Were they created for me? For you? Or were they created for someone else? Have they been updated? Do they make sense?

What are the rules? There seem to be a lot of them. When to do this and not to do that. This goes with this but not with that. Time to do XYZ but not ABC.

What are the rules?

If you really break it all down, rules are quite arbitrary. Sure, they may appear to instill peace and tranquility. But if you dig deep, they seem to keep us complacent. Comfortable. Calm. Orderly.

Orderly. Obedient.

Nothing wrong with that...unless those rules don't work for you. Unless they are good for someone else but not you. Now this may seem selfish and it should, but why should someone else come before you?

Is that selfish? Yes. And it's beautiful.

Start questioning the rules. Are they good for you? Are they working for you? Or are they keeping you trapped in a prison you never consciously agreed to?

#56 When Stuck, Shock The System

"Time to leave now, get out of this room, go somewhere, anywhere; sharpen this feeling of happiness and freedom, stretch your limbs, fill your eyes, be awake, wider awake, vividly awake in every sense and every pore."

Stefan Zweig

I had one client who was incredibly stuck in his life. No fun. He had one kid, a home, and a great job in the city. By all accounts, his life was set. But internally he was numb. He was absolutely stuck and didn't know what to do. He tried every technique under the sun. But everything he tried was simply a Band-Aid! It didn't actually change anything. A temporary fix. I knew exactly what we needed to do.

It was winter. We were at his home, working. I stopped. Told him to put on a bathing suit and grab a towel. He lived by the ocean and we were going in. The water at the time was about 45 degrees. There was snow on the ground.

He didn't actually believe me. I didn't explain. I didn't tell him the theory behind it. I couldn't feed that part of the brain that would have categorized fun into some kind of self-help solution. It would have rendered the whole thing ineffective.

"1, 2, 3," we screamed and ran into the ocean. It was like getting shocked with a 10,000-volt cattle prod. But in that moment, because the stuckness was caught by surprise, he woke the fuck up. It jarred him from his complacent sleep. Hell, it jarred me from my sleep. We stayed in the water for another ten minutes. We screamed. We breathed. We grounded. We made pledges to keep awakening. To keep having fun.

When we got out, the haze that had been over his eyes was gone. He was back. From that day forward he pledged to live. To breathe. To appreciate. To receive. To be.

He found himself.

If we start looking at our wellbeing as something that is imperative and not simply a luxury to be done when we have time, our lives will become much richer and deeper. We will engage something at the core of our being. It stimulates something inside and removes the mind from a habituated state of consciousness that is simply...kind of lame.

Now go find a damn cold body of water and howl!

#57 Find Your Tribe

"Don't waste your time being what someone wants you to become, in order to feed their list of rules, boundaries and insecurities. Find your tribe. They will allow you to be you, while you dance in the rain."

Shannon L. Alder

Author Sebastian Junger, in his book *Tribe* says, "We have a strong instinct to belong to small groups defined by clear purpose and understanding—'tribes.' This tribal connection has been largely lost in modern society, but regaining it may be the key to our psychological survival."

It is innate. It is how humans are wired. It is a very profound and beautiful quality about us sexy angels.

A tribe is not necessarily about comfort. It is about growth. It is about the discovery of Self. A tribe can push you. It can see your dark spots and call you out on them. The places where you hide.

The tribe is key when you need Truth. When you need to push through crap. When you need to roar.

The tribe will catch you when you fall. When you fail. When you quit.

The tribe is a place where vulnerability will soar. Where it is expected. Where it is respected.

The tribe is a thing of beauty. It ain't easy. It ain't always fun. But it is a form of standing up in the world.

It is power.

Find the tribe and become more.

IV. Your Freedom

#58 Feelings Are Your Superpower

"We are not thinking machines that feel, we are feeling machines that think."

António R. Damásio

Machines don't have feelings. Humans do. And we could all stand to feel a bit more.

I once worked with a brilliant woman. A pedigree of degrees from Harvard, Yale, and MIT. She was not only a lawyer but a doctor with a second doctorate on the way in psychology. When we started working together she already knew everything that was "wrong" with her. She had analyzed it from every angle her training would afford, which was quite extensive. As she told me when we first met, "I have daddy issues, mommy issues, I've studied Freud, and I work with the best psychologists in the field. I'm not sure you can possibly tell me anything new."

It was true, I couldn't tell her anything new. She knew it all. But how did she feel?

So, I asked her what she was feeling. Simply that. What was she feeling? She paused a few minutes and said she was stressed. I didn't respond immediately. Leaving space for her to feel that. Then she took a deep breath and said that she was actually feeling afraid.

Pause. Space. Room to feel.

I let her feel that. No analysis. No questioning. Just feeling.

And I asked her to let the mind go for a second and feel the fear. No judgment. No self-criticism. Just feel. And she did. And she cried.

Pause. Space. Room to feel.

She spoke again and said that life was so overwhelming and feels like she can't keep doing it. That a part of her just wanted to quit. Quit being the woman who needed to constantly win. Know it all. Fight.

Pause. Space. Room to feel.

She surrendered to that part. The part that had to have it all together. She cried even more. This time letting all control drop.

Pause. Space. Room to feel.

And that's when she saw it, she saw she was playing out a dynamic with her dad. A dynamic to prove her worth to him. One she had been doing throughout her entire life. Over and over again.

Pause. Space. Room to feel.

My client spent the rest of the session feeling, weeping, surrendering. When she was done she looked like someone who had just shed 50lbs off her shoulders. She was lighter. Still raw but relieved of the burden. She felt the truth. It was deeper than the machine could go. Deeper than the mind.

A machine understands the problem. It analyzes it. Compartmentalizes it. But we aren't machines. We are humans. And we humans feel the problem. And feeling is the key to freedom.

Pause. Space. Room to feel.

#59 It's Okay To Feel Like Pooh

*" 'I don't feel very much like Pooh today,' said Pooh.
'There, there,' said Piglet. 'I'll bring you tea and honey until
you do.'"*

A.A. Milne, Winnie the Pooh

Sometimes we have the fight.

Sometimes we don't.

Sometimes we surrender.

Sometimes we weep.

Sometimes we need more.

Sometimes we don't.

Sometimes it's fine to be just fine.

Thank goodness sometimes is just sometimes and not all of
the time.

#60 Feel It All

"After all, we humans are not just one thing, we are multiple things, all at once, and any man wearing a badge on his chest boasting one particular quality or value is a man who is hiding ten other qualities and values he didn't see fit to pin to his lapel."

Lenore Zion

Being married is the truest test of feeling multiple things at once. It still blows my mind. Loving someone so deeply and at the same time having the rage of a thousand burning suns. I mean, I don't feel that way toward my wife but I know others who do...

But it's important to remember that we can feel multiple things at once. It may not make sense to the brain, it doesn't have to. What is important is to be aware of it and allow it. You do not want to block it. That's just suppression.

Take for example, the heart.

It can ache. It can break. It can love. It can rage. It can dance. It can hate. It can shine.

It can do it all.

And that's the thing. It can do it all.

Sometimes all at once.

The more and more we become aware of our heart, the more empowering it is to feel deep fear and deep love at the same time. Blinding rage and blinding hope. Total loss and total connection.

Allow the heart to live the way it wants. Feel it all. It actually uncomplicates life. It's allowance.

It's like giving the heart some much needed air.

And from there, it will love in ways we've never known. Or maybe how we've always known but have just forgotten.

#61 You Are Magical

"Those who don't believe in magic will never find it."

Roald Dahl

I used to look up at the stars and wish upon them. No matter where I was in the world, I would find those stars and make a wish. But my most favorite time to make a wish was on Christmas Eve. That night holds a pregnant hush of magic that is bursting at the seams. It is like the heavens are waiting to grant that one wish, that one wish for that person who simply looks up and asks.

That's the thing about life, it is magical. Whether it is the night sky, Christmas Eve, a hug from your mom or dad, finding your path, or glimpsing a miracle. It is magical.

We are made up of stardust.

The human nose can detect up to 1 trillion smells.

Life is created in 9 months. An organ is built out of nothing to facilitate it. The baby breathes liquid.

Our bodies regulate with no conscious thought.

We are amazing creatures. We are phenomenal and exquisite works of art.

When life gets real. Let's take a deep breath and remember this.

Let's remember we are magical beings.

#62 Go Easy On Yourself

"Remember, you have been criticizing yourself for years and it hasn't worked. Try approving of yourself and see what happens."

Louise Hay

I am a glutton for self-hate. It is woven into the deep recesses of my being. It's gotten a lot better but she still rears her ugly head now and again.

I remember trying to learn pre-algebra in school. It was near impossible for me. I just couldn't get it. My mind didn't function that way.

Instead of getting help, I bashed myself. Profusely. After I received an exam with a low grade I would shred it. Annihilate it. I was disgusted. How could I be so stupid? How could I be so utterly mentally retarded? Why was I so useless?! After each test, I would go home, sit in the basement, watch around seven hours of television, and stuff my face with an entire package of Vienna Finger Cookies. I had to numb out.

14 years old and I was thinking those thoughts. Those ruthless judgments. It carried on for several decades.

Then at the time I started writing this blog, around my 34th birthday, I read the quote at the top of the previous page from Louise Hay. As simple as it was, it struck something deep. What if I didn't have to be my own worst enemy? What if I had my own back? What a concept. And so, slowly, I started having my back. I started to feel what it would be like to support myself. To cheer for myself. To encourage myself.

And you know what? It felt nice. It felt empowering. It felt…right.

We owe ourselves a level of civility that I don't think we often get...*from* ourselves. Civility *to* ourselves.

Compassion, kindness, holding, forgiveness, space. If we could give ourselves these things, our lives would be much quieter. Much simpler. Much more fun.

Civility towards oneself is one of the highest forms of love that I know.

Go easy on yourself. I am still learning but it is so much more enjoyable in the end. Besides, it's what I owe that 14-year-old boy.

#63 MEN, There Is No Shame In Asking For Help

"Ari?" My father's voice was soft.
"Ari, Ari, Ari. You're fighting this war in the worst possible way."
"I don't know how to fight it, Dad."
"You should ask for help," he said.
"I don't know how to do that, either."

Benjamin Alire Sáenz

As a man, "help" was always one of the hardest words for me. Near impossible.

It was a sign of weakness. Inadequacy. Stupidity. Being a pussy.

What if they took advantage of me in this vulnerable state? Used it against me? What if I lost my edge? My strength? My positioning in this relationship?

The thought alone would shut me down. A collapsing inward.

But the more I dove into the masculine, the more I found a completely different meaning of "help."

Strength, fellowship, power, acceptance, and growth. Rapid growth.

Why? If I wanted to achieve a goal, would I not do everything in my power to do just that? To shed any little egoic thought that blocked me from victory? Essentially, the smallness of male programming had to die. And is still dying. It doesn't give up that easily.

It is ludicrous to think I can do it alone. Or know it all, have all the answers, or excel at everything.

When I find myself asking for "help," I am utterly blown-away by the response. Usually a resounding YES. And if it's a NO, I admire that, because that "NO" person is owning their time and space.

The more "help" comes, the bigger leaps I can take. The more I can do what I want to do. The more my life becomes fluid and solid.

"Help," my dear men, is not weakness. It is strength beyond compare. It is masculinity at its finest.

#64 Dust Yourself Off And Get Back Up

"Why do we fall, sir? So that we can learn to pick ourselves back up."

Alfred J. Pennyworth

Here's the thing, we will fall. We will get back up. That is life.

I remember the worst breakup I have ever had. I fell down. Hard. It was the kind that cracked the heart in two.

My brother, my savior, drove all the way from Pittsburgh to Chicago and picked me up after it had happened. We drove back through the night. We pounded Red Bulls and double cheeseburgers from McDonalds. I wept and he listened. I screamed and he listened. I fell apart and he listened. I wouldn't have made it if it weren't for him. But you know what happened? I fell down and I got up. With help from him. My friends. My family. I never stop falling down. The key is how you get up.

Who will you surround yourself with to help you?

Fall down. Get up.

You don't have to do it alone. You don't have to suffer. You don't have to die. You don't even have to get up immediately.

But, let's be clear.

Fall down. Get up.

#65 Move Through The Quit

"When you go through a hard period, when everything seems to oppose you...when you feel you cannot even bear one more minute, NEVER GIVE UP! [emphasis mine] Because it is the time and place that the course will divert!"

Rumi

My very first day of orientation at the Department of Justice, my boss burst in and said, "We need to respond to the defense attorney on this drug case and it needs to be done today. Write it up." Then he left just as fast as he came in.

I'm pretty sure a piece of me died that moment. After all, I had never written a real response in my life. Let alone one that was crucial to a federal investigation of an international drug ring. My mind went blank with a system overload. The task was impossible.

I wanted to give up. The familiar feeling of quitting slowly crept over me. One that I knew oh so well.

It began with fear. Anxiety. Then my mind began rationalizing why I should quit. Finding reasons why it was necessary, for me, for my country!

But whispering in the background there was another feeling. A different feeling. One that I didn't know that well. It was a feeling of strength.

And then I remembered how hard I fought to get into the Department of Justice. How badly I wanted to be in the Narcotics Dangerous Drugs Division. How I called incessantly to get that job. And that's when I realized I couldn't quit. I wanted it. I asked for it. If I kept quitting in the middle of something difficult, something I ASKED for, I would probably never get anything or anywhere in my life.

So, I sat there. I breathed, pulled my head out of my ass, and went to work. I slept in the office that night, but I finished it.

When you don't quit, it is glorious. A piece of you strengthens. You learn more about who you are and where your limits are. You become invincible.

Pushing through may not be pretty, but it is worth it. It is your victory, and that can never be taken away.

#66 Find Your True North

"It takes courage to push yourself to places you have never been before...to test your limits...to break through barriers. And the day came when the risk it took to stay tight inside the bud was more painful than the risk it took to blossom."

Anaïs Nin

Your True North is essential in this life.

What is your True North? Well, that depends on each person.

Think of it as an anchor that you can always come back to. Something that grounds you, aligns you, helps you to see through the chaos.

It could be a symbol, a feeling, a knowing, a mantra, a picture, an idea, a principle, a declaration.

Whatever it is, it is important to have. Because as we go on this journey, we will be pushed, pulled, and thrown off course. We will forget. We will get lost. We will be persuaded. All...the...time.

But as long as we have that True North, we can always course-correct. That's why it's there.

Somewhere in this cosmic game, we knew life here on earth would be one hell of a ride and we would need something to remind us to stay the course.

Find True North. Let it evolve. Let it grow. Let it be seen.

For me, right now, it is my meditation. It is what gets me back to Truth. To the path. To me.

What's yours?

#67 A Barbie Does Not Define You

"Never be bullied into silence. Never allow yourself to be made a victim. Accept no one's definition of your life; define yourself."

Robert Frost

There once was this boy named Bryce. He was a sensitive boy. Had a twin sister that he loved very dearly. They played Barbies, My Little Pony, and had glittery stickers with bright colors.

Bryce loved spending time with his sister.

Until one day, Bryce met other boys his age. It was no longer just him and his twin sister.

The boys played with monster trucks. Liked this thing called Football. They spit. Lit things on fire. Punched.

A piece of Bryce loved being this kind of boy. Another piece of Bryce loved playing with his sister and their dolls.

He thought he could have it all! Bryce was wrong. Soon the boys made it very clear that playing with dolls was just for girls. That boys didn't play with those kinds of things. They were for sissies. Wimps. GIRLS!!!!

And somewhere deep down, Bryce listened. He let the dolls go and chose to only play with "boy things." He sure as heck wasn't going to be a girl!

GI Joe! Not Barbie.

But why? Both are plastic. Both have two legs and two arms. One has a gun. Another has fun. He loved them both. He loved shooting and destroying things. He also loved playing in the DreamHouse with Ken.

Ahhh, but that is how our culture works. It ruthlessly splits things right down the middle. We see it in religion. Politics. Race. Sex.

It's a brilliant way of control. But when you break this split down to its essence, we can see how patently absurd it is. How fear-based it is. How the foundational tenets on which each of these institutions bases their belief systems are simply insane.

When we look real close, there is no split. The labels and definitions are completely arbitrary. They actually do not exist.

A doll is a doll. A life is a life.

And you get to have it all.

No splits.

#68 Judgment Ends When We Stop Judging

"It is not the actions of others which trouble us (for those actions are controlled by their governing part), but rather it is our own judgments."

Marcus Aurelius

I'm pretty sure we all experience judgment. I think it's one of those things that no one escapes. And judgment is crushing. It clamps down on our life force and results in stuckness. An immovable weight that most of us have to battle against.

Sometimes it is small. Sometimes it is big. Regardless, it is unnecessary. It is a form of suffering.

Now, the funny thing is that judgment starts with us. The insidious fear of judgment begins with judgment of ourselves.

Let's break it down:

1. If you fear judgment from others, it is because you judge YOURSELF for that thing.

   a. Ex: You are worried people will criticize you when you give your presentation. That's because you are already criticizing yourself before and during your presentation. You then project that fear onto others, regardless if they are actually judging,

2. If you fear judgment from others, it is because you are judging OTHERS for that thing.

   a. Ex: You worry people won't like your wildly fantastic and fierce shirt. That is because you judge others who wear their versions of wildly fantastic and fierce shirts. Find where you judge others for the thing you fear most about being judged for yourself.

Judgment ends when we stop judging ourselves and others. It's quite simple actually. Find where you do it and why you do it, and choose to end it. You don't deserve it and neither do they. It's so deceivingly simple in its beauty.

#69 Your Weakness Is Your Strength

"Every weakness contains within itself a strength."

Shusaku Endo

"It's not working. I feel like an impostor. They'll figure me out. Before every meeting I am anxious and it's draining. I'm working with the CEO directly, and I feel fucked."

This was what came out of the mouth of my client. This person is phenomenal. Natural instincts. A real know-how of the world. Street smart. But was told a long time ago he had a learning disability. That the way he learned was slow and unproductive. And it has haunted him ever since. Thus, impostor syndrome.

What did we do? We turned the story on its head and made his "disability" a weapon.

First, we identified where he had succeeded. What he was naturally good at. Turns out he liked building stuff for people. Loved visualizing and figuring out their "why" for building. He once built a kitchen island for his mother. He did it from a place of giving. He dove into it out of curiosity.

He planned it out in his head. He wanted to get crystal clear on what his mom wanted and how he could deliver. He was excited. And that's how he learned. That's how he worked. And that was HIS style of working.

And so, we reverse engineered that to apply to his job. Instead of trying to sell or be perfect, he began by asking questions. He began to become curious about the needs of his clients. There was no pressure because it was a genuine wanting to know. "What do you want and how can I provide that for you?"

From there, he built. He created. He delivered.

So, we boiled his style of learning and doing down to a few bullet points:

1. He needs to feel a connection to the WHY of his client.

2. He needs to genuinely want to help.

3. He needs to have enough information gathered to begin to build.

4. He needs to be prepared enough to feel confident.

5. He needs to feel that he embodies the project as opposed to just another check for the boss.

If he didn't have these points met, he wouldn't care and would struggle.

He left our session in tears. Not because of me but because he didn't know he was allowed to learn this way. That he could use his "disabilities" as strengths. He didn't know what his damn gifts were!

This session took 40 minutes. In 40 minutes we uncovered 30 years of judgment, mislearning, a presumed disability, and what his superpowers were. It may be that quick. It doesn't have to take years.

I say this because at the end of the day, we all need help. Eric Schmidt of Google said, "If you are looking to grow and be at the top of your game, get a coach. Seriously."

We can't know it all. And what scares me is the latent power most of us have that is hidden by some unknown program that blocks us from embodying a completely different level of living. It not only scares me, but it pisses me off.

We should all be the commanders of our lives.

Big, bold, and beautiful. It is not a weakness or disability. It is a strength waiting to be unlocked.

#70 Vulnerability Is Powerful

"Out of your vulnerabilities will come your strength."

Sigmund Freud

Merriam-Webster Dictionary's definition of Vulnerable:
1 : capable of being physically or emotionally wounded
2 : open to attack or damage : vulnerable to criticism

That definition, wow. Really makes you want to be vulnerable. A little fucked up, isn't it? Vulnerability is not a weakness: it is in fact the opposite. It is core. It is power.

Yes, vulnerability is power.

When we have fully entered into our vulnerability, we are untouchable. Brené Brown, the queen of vulnerability, sums it up perfectly, "Vulnerability sounds like truth and feels like courage. Truth and courage aren't always comfortable, but they're never weakness."

Truth and courage, let that sit there for a moment. Truth being exactly what we're feeling in that moment with no protection. No defenses. No guards up. It is the rawest, purest, TRUEST self. It is our Truth in that moment. And it is the Courage to stand in it. Not shutting it down. Not running from it. Not hiding. To embody it, front and center, baring your expression of self for the world to see. That is no small feat. Especially since we are told by society that vulnerability means you will be stabbed by an adorable French bulldog while unconditionally loving it.

So, why is it so difficult? Because getting there can appear to hurt. It's scary. It makes us feel things we don't want to feel. See things we don't want to see. For me, vulnerability has been one of the hardest things to embrace in my life. For many people, the word immediately brings up judgments like weak, soft, hopeless, unproductive, ineffective, worthless. As one client said, "If I open to it, I'll be blubbering pool of mush all day. No thank you." That's what we are up against when we decide to go into vulnerability.

But, to me, vulnerability is the entry point into EVERYTHING. It brings humility, sincerity, honesty, Truth, strength, responsibility, and presence. Going forward, in any situation, when you feel stuck or trapped, go back to the definition from Brené Brown "...sounds like truth and feels like courage." Are you being truthful about how you really feel and are you courageous enough to feel it? From there you can honestly become anything in any situation.

Vulnerability no longer equals death; it equals life.

#71 Dancing Is A Cure

"Sometimes letting things go is an act of far greater power than defending or hanging on."

Eckhart Tolle

I felt stuck during this one particular week. Almost like an energetic constipation. Nothing I did could get me unstuck. So, I had to shock the system. I did the one thing I knew would make me so uncomfortable that it would dislodge my stuckness: go dancing.

I am not a dancer.

Never been a dancer. Hate it. So, I tried a form that would really shake it up, contact improv. This is dancing with people you physically touch and essentially roll your body weight against in a dance of balance and surrender. Your body becomes their body.

Not. My. Comfort. Zone.

So I went, and as I sat there, melting down inside, a guy came over and asked if I would like to dance. A guy. Another man!

Not. My. Comfort. Zone.

I told him this was new to me. He told me not to worry, but this was the advanced class. Ooops. I asked if he could show me to the beginner's class. None existed. I almost vomited. He reached for my hand and I grabbed it. We began the dance.

Not. My. Comfort. Zone.

Let's break this down. Here I was, dancing with a man. Not triggering at all to my years of masculinity conditioning (it was triggering!)...Moving my body against his, trying to release and anticipate his weight through free flow. All the while desperately attempting to surrender my body to let an instinctual movement take over. Most of which goes against decades of my normal, rigid, Bryce movement.

Not. My. Comfort. Zone.

How long did I last? A few minutes? Half hour?

Two hours. Two hours with this guy. Moving. Trusting. Freaking out. Trusting. Learning. Surrendering. Freaking out. Opening. Freaking out. Repeat. Over and over.

By the time I was done, I didn't know who I was. I had bonded with this man. My body moved with his. I trusted him. I thanked him. He was so patient. So kind. He allowed me to be vulnerable and imperfect. He embraced my fears and stayed with me for two long hours.

I woke up the next morning unstuck. There was no strategy. No planning. I simply knew that if I wanted to get unstuck, I would need to go where I've never gone before.

Try it. Find that thing. Don't wait. Don't strategize. Don't give into the stuckness.

Find your Dance!

#72 There Is No Tiger

"When life itself seems lunatic, who knows where madness lies? Perhaps to be too practical is madness. To surrender dreams—this may be madness. Too much sanity may be madness—and maddest of all: to see life as it is, and not as it should be!"

Miguel de Cervantes Saavedra

We all react. Completely normal. To a partner. A boss. A situation. A result. A word. A look.

We react. It makes sense. It is our primal nature. A lion! Fear. A pterodactyl! Hide.

These instincts are us. The problem is that they are being triggered all of the time. Our nervous systems can't distinguish between an "urgent work project" and the threat of a lion. Fight or flight!

And since we are reacting all of the time, we have a tendency to be triggered more than ever. This ever-present, low-level fear. Anxiety. Life in peril. Waiting. Watching. Anticipating the next threat.

This is extremely destructive. It means we are never truly present. We are always projecting into the future. There is no NOW. There is rarely satisfaction in the moment.

What do we do?

At some level we must surrender to the present. There is no way around it. It may be uncomfortable. It may feel unsafe. It may feel unproductive. But engaging the now and fully participating in it is one of the most powerful things we can do.

It requires patience. Persistence. Practice.

Now is the time.

Quick exercise: Take a few deep breaths. See what you're feeling. Drop the thoughts and stories. What is present for you in this moment? What are you seeing with your two eyes in this moment? What does your chair feel like? What do your clothes feel like? What do you feel like? Are you big and spacious? Or are you contracted? Are you hungry? Are you reacting? If so, to what? Is there a pit in your stomach? Or is there gratitude? Do you feel like something is about to come at you or are you charging forward in a decisive, present manner?

There is no lion. There is only now.

#73 You Will Be Tested

"There are moments when troubles enter our lives and we can do nothing to avoid them.
But they are there for a reason.
Only when we have overcome them will we understand why they were there."

Paulo Coelho

I do believe that when you decide to shift something in your life, you will be tested.

I have yet to see an instance where it didn't happen.

Let me share a story. One that my wife hates. One that I do hope she does not read. I'm pretty sure she won't make it this far into the book anyway.

The story begins many moons ago when I was living with my brother in NYC. It was a glorious time. We were kings!

But alas, his time had come and he was moving in with his girlfriend, soon-to-be wife. This left a vacant room for me to find a roommate. So, I put up an ad on Craigslist for the summer before my lease expired. I got many inquiries but one in particular stood out.

It was from two female Swedish exchange students studying fashion who wanted to rent my spare room. They were going to share a full-size air mattress. They liked to party. They were easy going and were extremely friendly. They were looking to have a summer of fun…

Let me get this straight, two Swedish exchange students sharing a bed who wanted to party all summer staying in my apartment. Hahaha, God had answered my prayers!

But there was a hiccup. I had a girlfriend. We were getting serious. Right on that cusp of real commitment. And there was my test. Would I choose a summer of unfettered Swedish orgy or this cusp of a girlfriend?

You will be tested when it matters most. A lifetime of partnership or a two-month hedonistic summer? Make no mistake about it. It may come in any form. But it will hit your weakest spot. The most brutal part of yourself. Mine was commitment. Well, commitment and Swedish orgies.

Fast forward ten years later and that girlfriend became my wife.

Choose wisely.

#74 Trust Your Voice By Listening To It

"To be nobody-but-yourself—in a world which is doing its best, night and day, to make you everybody else—means to fight the hardest battle which any human being can fight; and never stop fighting."

E.E.. Cummings

I was listening to the Noah Kagan podcast and he was interviewing author and entrepreneur, Keith Ferrazzi.

Noah: How do you know when you've made the right decision?

Keith: With this question...have you perfected the ability to trust what voice you listen to?

Noah: How do you do that?

Keith: Practice.

There it is. Practice listening to the right voice.

And that's it. What voice to listen to. Some people are extremely clear with the voices they listen to. Their gut. Their instinct. That deep-down knowing.

I, on the other hand, have never trusted mine. It's dramatic. It's full of false starts. It's mixed with the voices of my family, friends, and society. Hell, I have a twin sister whose voice I definitely hear in my head.

But, through practice, this voice will become clearer. It becomes a core knowing. It starts pulling in a different direction. A direction of truth.

This knowing grows. And so did my path. Soon it led to a relentless hunt for more of this voice.

The job is knowing which voice to listen to. Knowing which path to follow. KNOWING is the key. It does not matter what job you have, where you come from, who you do or do not have in your life, it is your voice and your voice alone that will carry you through the darkest times and to the highest highs.

Because once you find that voice, you will most likely realize it is connected to something much, much bigger than we could ever imagine.

#75 Fun Is Absofuckinglutely Necessary

"It ain't no fun if the homies can't have none."

Snoop Dogg

Growing up in Greensburg, Pennsylvania, we were surrounded by farmland. Acres and acres of beautiful farmland as far as the eye could see. It was the home to magic, fireflies, forests, earthy smells, and possibility.

My friends owned the largest farm in the area, and in highschool we made good use of it.

On the weekends we would build great big bonfires on the top of a hill hidden by trees. We would dance, sing, drink, and be wild animals into the night. We had epic water balloon fights under the moon. Hours of capture the flag—hiding in the deep, fragrant grass. We would stargaze on the roofs of our cars. We jumped off barn rafters 20 feet high into enormous piles of hay. Maybe we would find love that night. Oftentimes not. But we were friends. We felt alive. We had each other and nothing else really mattered.

Our imagination and quest for the next fun adventure was one of the greatest periods in my life.

We didn't ask for permission. We didn't justify it. We just did it because we wanted to. Our time was ours and ours alone. Fun.

Then we got older. We became "responsible." We became lawyers, doctors, engineers, bosses, family men. And slowly but surely that fun began to die. We had obligations. We had rules and restrictions. Fun was a luxury. One that was only "earned" after a long week of working. Fun was no longer a priority.

This happens to most people. Very rare is there someone who escapes this transition. And even rarer is the person who doesn't suffer from it.

In myself and in my clients, I notice that when this carefree, fun, adventurous side is crushed or neutered, we begin to feel that dissatisfaction. The schism begins to show. Resentment, frustration, and numbness begin to be the new norm. More fears, more anxieties, more caring what others think.

Fun isn't a luxury. It is a necessity. It is an absofuckinglutely necessity. It is an essential component of being human. It is our fuel to creativity. To love. It feeds the soul. It feeds our joy. It feeds our curiosity.

It jumpstarts our lives. It makes life worth living. It reignites dormant flames. It is the part at the time of our death that says, "Wow! What a ride!"

Find the fun in life!

#76 Gratitude Transcends Barriers

"We can complain because rose bushes have thorns, or rejoice because thorns have roses."

Alphonse Karr

I was working with a consulting team and we were having a roundtable to discuss why they were all in a mental rut. Each was burnt out and no one really could focus on the intense work that was required of them.

As we sat there, I said very little. I wanted to see who would speak first. A young man from India was the first to break the silence. He said that he for one was very grateful to be there. He had grown up very poor in a part of rural India where there was no running water. He had to bike ten miles to the closest internet cafe.

We were all silent.

He went on explaining how he knew that if he didn't teach himself how to use a computer, he would die in that tiny village, poor and hungry. What he did was unthinkable. The lengths to which he went to educate himself. To fight to get into college. To rise to the top of his class. Often going to bed hungry or not having shelter before an exam.

And here we were. The 47th floor of a posh building with all the amenities. No expense spared.

We were all silent.

He said, "I am grateful to have this current problem with all of you."

I am grateful to have this current problem with all of you. What a statement.

And that's when everything shifted.

Eventually, the whole team went around saying what they were grateful for and why. Real gratitude. Not just lip service.

The group spoke of everything that had been difficult in their lives. Divorce, death, miscarriage, accidents, and abuse. But for that moment, they all were all grateful. To have space. Silence. A listening ear. Care. Understanding. Empathy. A voice.

The gratitude came not from comparing who had it worse. Or about "children are starving in Africa" type gratitude. Rather it was perspective as it came to their lives. To that moment of time for them. It was a rare and special moment. One I am eternally grateful for.

Find the real gratitude and it will change you.

#77 Say, "I'm Sorry."

"You never really understand a person until you consider things from his point of view...until you climb inside of his skin and walk around in it."

Harper Lee

One of the most important lessons of them all.

A while back, a very good friend of mine scalped himself. Literally. He caught his head on a piece of metal and cut deeply into his scalp to the point where you could lift the skin flap up. Needless to say, this was not a good situation.

We Ubered over to the nearest clinic to get this remedied ASAP. When we pulled up to the clinic, I flung open the door to help my buddy, who was in shock. The door bumped another car door beside us. I barely noticed. It looked like a clunker. We were in mission mode and this was no time to stop.

As we crossed the street, rushing to get him inside, we heard a man yelling behind us. We turned around and there was a guy screaming at us to go back and speak to him.

Supposedly, we did him wrong. I had no clue what he was talking about. We kept going, ignoring him.

We got situated inside and I saw this guy coming at us through the window of the clinic. Now I'm getting pissed. I have a scalped friend bleeding beside me and some NY crazy storming at us. Instead of having him come into the clinic and create chaos, I decided I would meet him outside so my buddy was safe and could be taken care of.

When I got outside, there in front of me was a gigantic man. I'm 6'1" but this man had to be 6'6" and about a solid 350 pounds. My only goal was to keep this guy out of the clinic. Then he laid into me. "You fucked my car up. What the fuck. That's my fucking car. You fucking disrespect my shit. You're fucking bullshit. Disrespecting my shit."

I was pretty sure I was going to have to fight this guy or at least attempt to fight him before his fist imploded my face. But when I heard him say "disrespect," something pinged inside me. Amongst the blinding rage and fear, I caught that one word. It hit me, this guy feels like he was disrespected by two punk asses who were trying to run off.

And out of my mouth came two solitary words: "I'm sorry." I said it again, "I'm sorry. I truly am."

Then I repeated his word, "I meant no disrespect. My friend had a major head injury and to tell you the truth, I'm scared.

This is the first time I've seen this and I have no idea what to do but get him in that clinic. I'm sorry."

I was vulnerable. I was real. It's all I could do.

The guy pauses. Stares at me. I stare at him. And he says, "Thank you."

What?

I was dumbfounded. Absolutely dumbfounded. He then went on to say he knows shit like this can be tough and we gotta watch out for family. And said thank you again. Took BOTH my hands in his and held them and shook them praying for my friend.

Then he smiled, turned around, and left. I stood there in complete disbelief. What had just happened?

He simply wanted an acknowledgement. An apology. To be seen. To be heard. Probably a man that has been disrespected a lot in his life. Probably tired of people treating him and his property as second-class.

That's the funny thing about us humans, we all feel. We all want to be understood. We don't want to be disrespected. We want to be heard. And by truly hearing what the other person is saying, underneath the yelling, underneath the hurt, we are all people wanting that acknowledgement. And in this case it was,

"I'm sorry."

Conclusion: We Have Reached The...Beginning?

"Jesus Christ knew he was God. So wake up and find out eventually who you really are. In our culture, of course, they'll say you're crazy and you're blasphemous, and they'll either put you in jail or in a nut house (which is pretty much the same thing). However if you wake up in India and tell your friends and relations, 'My goodness, I've just discovered that I'm God,' they'll laugh and say, 'Oh, congratulations, at last you found out.'"

Alan W. Watts

And here we are, the end...or the beginning? What a life this is. To realize everything matters and nothing matters. To realize this is all a giant paradox. We are both light and dark. A wonderful, fucked-up amalgamation of brilliance. That there is no right way to do it. No need to compare or judge. No need to choose anything that goes against yourself. No need to perpetuate some false reality of yourself that leads to suffering. No need!

This isn't said in some pedantic and trite way but as Truth. A deep knowing of Truth that we all share deep in the bowels of our souls. A deep knowing that somewhere we were once whole but got off track. We started buying into some other reality that was not our own. A deep knowing that the real reality is far greater than any contrived one. One where we are able to conquer the limitations of the mind and subconscious belief systems that steer us away from ourselves. Where we can do this with vulnerability, integrity, and fortitude. That it will not separate us from the rest of the world but bring us closer.

And this closeness will satisfy something within us. A satisfaction that cannot be born from an external source but rather from the profound realization of the magnitude of who we are. Not a schism, but possibility. A wellspring of possibility.

But to tap into that possibility, it takes courage. It takes courage to peer into the abyss and admit to ourselves that something is off. Something isn't quite right in life. Even though it may be easier to remain asleep, in its safety and comfort, it's just not right. And we acknowledge that.

We acknowledge our humanness. We embrace it. Over and over again.

And that's the next step—to know we must repeat it all over and over and over again. Whatever "it" is. It may be the need to deconstruct more blockages. To see false identities. To chip away at places where we close our hearts and our voices. To stand up more. To not fall for the false narratives of society. To choose ourselves. To choose over and over again.

It doesn't end. And why should it? The need to grow and change should be a constant. This is where a lot of self-help falls flat. A lot of it makes you think that once you achieve a certain level that you're done. Incorrect. That means you are settling for that level. As if it's the end. Who wants to settle? My meditation teacher always says, "Today's awakening is tomorrow's sleep." It's just like working out. Where once we could do three push ups we can now do ten. Let's go for more. Let's push the limits of everything in our lives. Let's grow. Let's be more.

In Case of Emergency is about you. About getting what you need. It's about breaking the damn glass!

I leave you with an aspirational quote for all of us embarking on this ride. Much, love. Bryce

"A kind of light spread out from her. And everything changed color. And the world opened out. And a day was good to awaken to. And there were no limits to anything. And the people of the world were good and handsome.

And I was not afraid anymore."

John Steinbeck

About the Author

Bryce Kennedy is a former corporate attorney who worked for the Department of Justice, Senate Judiciary Committee, F.I.M.R.C., and Sullivan & Cromwell LLP.

Currently, Bryce's main focus is the deep study of meditation. He has spent the last 6 years training with the teachings and techniques of Samuel Sagan, at the Clairvision School of Meditation.

In addition, Bryce lectures and coaches with individuals and companies like P&G, Spotify, Lululemon, Squarespace, Athleta, ViacomCBS, and WeWork. He was the in-house coach for the Boston Consulting Group in New York City.

He has been writing a daily motivational blog since 2014 called The Daily Boom and was published by PureWow, Thrive Global, Reader's Digest, Do the Good Stuff, and Whale Bone Magazine.

Bryce Kennedy currently lives in Brooklyn, NY, with his wife. They don't have a cat, yet. Yet...

You can find Bryce at:

www.brycekennedy.co